BRANDPSYCHO

A psychological exposé into
the hidden side of branding
(and how to not turn into a brand yourself.)

MAX JAKOB LUSENSKY

Black Books Publishing
Richardstraße 73/74,
120 53 Berlin, Germany

jakob@lusensky.com
www.brand-psycho.com

1st Edition published 2016 by The Zurich Laboratory
2nd Edition Published 2018 by Black Books Publishing

Editing: C. Claudia Galego

ISBN: 9781717890733

CONTENTS

It is now clear to me that there was no difference between our behaviour and that of people in a madhouse; but at the time I only dimly suspected this and, like all madmen, I thought everyone was mad except myself.

– Leo Tolstoy, "A Confession"[i]

PROLOGUE

I wanted this story to begin in Tokyo, for it to be about how I, Jakob Lusensky, the hidden persuader, high on success on the forty-eighth floor of a Tokyo skyscraper, suddenly have a revelation. The earth starts rumbling and the building shakes. My heart is racing as I am thrown from the glass window. Dressed in a white shirt and black tie, I fall in slow motion, cool beats accompanying my descent to the ground. I wanted this dramatic narrative, told with strong emotion, to illustrate the fall of the modern-day madman. It was to be a personal confession, rich in metaphor in order to stir mystery around my person and hopefully kidnap your imagination. I wanted to be your hero. I wanted you to love me, and the technique I wanted to use is the same technique used by brands on the marketplace. I was still thinking and acting like a brand myself.

Back then, in the midst of a rising Arab Spring, as Steve Jobs put away his sneakers for good and

Starbucks Coffee decided to drop the company name in its logotype, my fantasies were caught up in the same narrative structures as were the brands I'd set out to criticize. I had merely shifted sides in the same story. The marketer, helping global companies brand their products successfully, had turned to his shadow side, the anti-heroic rebel attacking the very companies that had fed him. I was still animated by that same heroic myth, still under the spell of the brands feeding my rebellious attitude—still trying to occupy a position in the marketplace, that is, inside your mind.

Today things are somewhat different. I have settled into a more paradoxical relationship to brands. The love-hate relationship has cooled off and I can appreciate how the pseudo-symbols of the marketplace have helped me become more aware of my desires and needs. I have come to see the most popular brands in our culture today as mirrors of our *zeitgeist*. They embody the spirit of our time, the ideas, ideals, and values to which we collectively aspire. If we analyze the underlying fantasies in the stories brands tell us, and reflect critically on their related images, we can observe how our individual—and our culture's—innermost yearnings unfold.

In this book I tell four different stories rooted in a process I have named "de:branding." It is a process engaged in better understanding what we project culturally and individually onto brands—such as the world's most admired consumer icon, Apple Inc. In the Apple brand, we notice at play contemporary culture's search for magic and transcendence through technology. We observe Steve Jobs turned magician and tech-messiah in a culture obsessed with visual communication. We see how our deepest needs for self-realization are projected onto our latest gadgets, that our favorite tech toys keep us preoccupied in a bid to help us escape the mundane reality of our lives as mortals. We are asked to hold life to its surfaces—to keep surfing—as we continue to mirror ourselves in their enchanted screens.

The owls are not what they seem to be

No, there was never any revelation in Tokyo, and I was not dressed like Don Draper in the TV series *Mad Men*. In reality there were fewer contrasts; there was more mystery. It was more an episode of *Twin Peaks* than *Mad Men*: a slow, dreamlike, surreal unfolding of the person behind the mask that I had taken for being myself. It was a curious dance that shifted my attention from waking life realities to my own dreams, where "the owls are not what they seem to be."[ii] A sense of selfhood was awakened in my separation from marketplace fantasies and return to my own imagination.

No, I never fell through the window, but rather followed the green fire-exit sign and started walking the long way down the spiral stairway, forty-eight floors. Round and round and round, slowly I began to spin out of the web I had woven around myself, to emerge from my "branded self," and with it, a life lived transiently, always on the move, too high up, transcending country lines. I was inflated by lofty ideas and aspirations while feeling sickened by the possibilities offered me. I did not wake up until I met the gods out on the street.

Gods have become diseases, have become brands

One of the founding fathers of depth psychology, Carl Gustav Jung, once wrote that "[t]he gods have become diseases; Zeus no longer rules Olympus but rather the solar plexus, and produces curious specimens for the doctor's consulting room."[iii] By this he meant that our individual anxieties, panic attacks, mood swings, compulsions, and somatic symptoms are not simply psychological problems in need of diagnosis. They can and should be seen as a call from powers beyond our conscious control inviting us to change. In this (for some) esoteric promise, we encounter an idea Jung held in common with Sigmund Freud, which is that we individuals are not entirely the masters of our own houses. The poet W.H. Auden wrote, "We are lived by powers we pretend to understand."[iv] Or in other words, human motivation is always unconscious. Seen in this way, it is not by escaping, trying to rid ourselves of, or fixing psychological symptoms that we develop and change. The possibility of transformation presents itself when we go where it hurts, by facing our depression and anxiety, our mortality. By penetrating more deeply into our symptoms and carefully listening to their messages, we can open ourselves to the evolution of a new life path.

Today these gods, as well as their diseases, are alive and kicking not only inside of us but also on the marketplace. Our most beloved brands are psychic forces sometimes as powerful and real as the gods we once believed in. Our relationship to their ideals and images shapes our individual psyches as well as some of the cultural pathologies of our time. Brands today go well beyond their logotypes and have, in our postmodern era, transformed into psychic entities and powerful pseudo-symbols. Teeming with contradictions, they seem to carry the potential to make us as sick as they promise to make us happy.

Apple. Starbucks. Nike. Understood psychologically, de:branded, brands that once represented powerful addictions can be transmuted into Trojan horses that help us break into our individual and cultural needs and desires. With a better understanding of our relationship to these brands and the stories they tell us, we can, paradoxically, open ourselves up to a new story for our own lives. But first let us learn how to de:brand.

De:branding

Like hackers, we need to read code, in this case the code of a brand. The code of a brand, the stories it tells via mass and social media, can be said to follow certain archetypal structures or root metaphors. Archetypes are universal narratives of expression associated with ideas and images that can be found in myths, legends, folktales, and religions across cultures and generations. They can also be found in the stories brands tell us. Today, the process of marketing works on this level, which I refer to as *mythos*. By critically yet playfully decoding the complex of images, texts, and emotional ideas with which a brand charges its communications, we can begin to de:brand it. If instead we remain unaware of the psychological and mythological dimensions of brands, we risk having our emotions held captive by them, or more pessimistically, being coopted by them into a colonized psychological state in which a part of our self, a part of our desires, stays projected onto their shiny surfaces.

Starbucks Coffee, when de:branded, reveals itself to be more than a supplier of our daily roast. Psychologically, on the level of *mythos*, the brand can be said to embody the omnipresent, nourishing, but also potentially devouring Great Mother archetype, with its associated imagery and ideas. Starbucks promises to satisfy our oral desires and other needs for mothering—as long as we continue believing its myth. Undressed, stripped of its clothes, Starbucks presents the ambiguous face of the siren, the devious temptress leading men to shipwreck: the face it uses as its logotype. The song that Starbucks sings for the collective is seductive yet sad: a hymn to the uprooted post-modern nomad longing nostalgically, like Odysseus, for home.

Branded or de:branded? We are left with an existential choice either to continue to project our soul's needs onto the mirrors of the marketplace or to start withdrawing some of our projections. The latter process is enabled by a change in attitude that transforms brands from symbols of desire into mirrors for self-reflection. Paradoxically, what brands offer us is an invitation to reflect psychologically on our own individual and cultural wants and needs. Today's visual culture can help us to understand how deeply psychic our so-called objective reality actually is.

What is asked of us, perhaps, is that we

become political not only by "Occupying Wall Street," but by occupying our own psyche—that we foster a symbolic understanding of the images, products, and lifestyles that surround us, and better understand how brands, mass media, popular culture, and individual psychology have become interwoven today. An archetypal perspective like this can help penetrate brands' glossy surfaces and the ideas, ideals, and aspirations we unconsciously project onto them. With the help of this lens, we can see how brands, as the gods of today's marketplace, play the role of the protagonist in the dominant mythological drama of our time—that of globalization.

Such a change in perspective is a potentially subversive act—a silent protest, foremost not through rebellion but reflection. It seeks not rhetoric but imagination, empathy, and resilience. Such a symbolic understanding of the reality that surrounds us can also help free psychology from its obsession with the individual, and help psychology become interested in culture and the collective again. When we start to reflect more intently on our desire for mothering by the marketplace, our search for instant gratification in consumption, and our narcissistic need for fulfillment through technology, we can break our identification with the persona of our branded selves—the collective aspirations, images, and ideals that brands advocate through their stories—stories we have for too long assumed to be our own.

How not to read this book

This introduction is the closest this book comes to any program, method, or technique. The following pages contain a collection of four essays (herein book chapters) written during my psychoanalytical training in Zürich, Switzerland. They were written separately and I have no intention of imposing an overarching narrative or interpretive structure. The first essay, "Our Modern Market in Search of Soul," explores the pseudo-spiritual foundation of today's marketplace. It presents you with the evil twin brother of Jung, the psycho-anarchist Otto Gross, and tells the story of a marketplace seemingly searching for soul while offering a new type of enchanted consumerism.

The second essay, "The Brand Complex," gives the what, why, and how of branding viewed through a psychoanalytical lens. It explores the idea of the branded self. It compares brands to psychological complexes, discusses the process of projection, and tells the story of an American UFO cult and what we can learn from the failure of its prophecy.

The last two essays of this book can be seen as case studies on how to de:brand consumer icons. The third essay, "Did You Bite the Magic Apple?", tries to better understand the myth that radiates in the background story told by the world's most admired brand. It finds the seeds of Apple Inc.'s mythology and parts of its success in the psychology of Steve Jobs, the messiah of the millennium generation. It explores how a belief in magic is invoked in those of us who use the company's products and continue to bite the magic Apple.

Finally, in the ethnological experiment "The Myth of Starbucks," an essay written during a field study spanning eight weeks at various Starbucks coffee houses around Europe, I turn to another of the most beloved brands of our time, reading it as a Trojan horse for breaking into not only Starbucks, but our globalized culture as such. I look at how our ideals and aspirations, along with our own unmet yearning for mothering, community, and home, are projected onto its siren symbol. We find that both brands—Apple and Starbucks—can be imagined as reenactments of age-old myths in the arena of the marketplace. And, as with all myths yet to be unveiled, we live them today as though they were true.

1
OUR MODERN MARKET
IN SEARCH OF SOUL

In his monumental address "Science as a Vocation," delivered at Munich University in 1918, social scientist Max Weber proclaimed the modern world "disenchanted": "One need no longer have recourse to magical means in order to master or implore the spirits, as did the savage, for whom such mysterious powers existed."ᵛ For Weber, technology had brought humankind closer to the workings of the world, thereby freeing it from religious superstitions and magical beliefs. But as Weber was busy "demystifying" our Western world, three hundred kilometers southeast of Munich, another great thinker of the twentieth century was in the process of doing something quite the opposite.

Carl Gustav Jung had drawn the same conclusions as Weber: modern life was disenchanted, stripped of meaning and mystery. But as the psychiatrist he was, Jung went one step further in also prescribing a remedy for this diagnosis. In the same year that Weber addressed his Munich audience, Jung shared, in the preface to his essay "On the Psychology of the Unconscious," his own reflections on the First World War and the attitude he saw needed. "Individual self-exploration, return of the individual to the ground of human nature, to his own deepest being with its individual and social destiny—here is the beginning of a cure for that blindness which reigns at the present hour."[vi] He proposed that the modern person "turn inward" toward psyche and soul, where a symbolically meaningful life could still be found. He called for a process of personal re-enchantment embedded with the political promise of collective change: one individual at a time.

Jung spoke from personal experience. He had just come out of a "creative illness"[vii] initiated by his break with Sigmund Freud, a separation that had taken him on a Homeric odyssey into the depths of his psyche, an experience that would heavily influence his own version of psychoanalysis. He would later write about the importance of this period: "Everything later was merely the outer classification, scientific elaboration, and the integration into life."[viii] He had discovered a "constructive method" of self-exploration that seemed to offer the potential for personal transformation—a method involving a radical shift in attitude in light of which the spiritual needs of humanity came to be seen as central to healing. Did this method not also promise to return mystery and re-enchantment to the life of the modern person?

This is one of the questions I set out to explore in this chapter, in which I hope to offer an alternative viewpoint to the idea of our modern world as disenchanted. Today, a hundred years since Weber proclaimed modernity in Munich, it is often claimed that we live in a demystified secular world driven by "economical man" and his rational needs. This is not completely true, and following the arguments of thinkers such as sociologist Zygmunt Bauman,[ix] I would like to sketch an alternative story about the re-enchantment of our modern world; about the projection onto the pseudo-substitutes offered by today's marketplace of humanity's "religious instinct," which Jung connected to in the depths of his own psyche; indeed, about the integration of magic and mystery into the market's "spiritual interiority." Along the way, I hope also to illuminate how Jung's ideas about self-realization and building a religion of individual character have been led astray, incorporated subliminally into today's psychological economy.

Brandpsycho

Experiments in enchantment

Jung was far from alone in experimenting with new re-enchantment techniques in the Weimar Era following the end of the First World War. In Zürich, the Dada movement, elaborating wildly with art, dance, and poetry, rejected reason and prized nonsense, intuition, and the irrational. This cultural phenomenon was initially regarded with interest by Jung, but he quickly rejected it as "too idiotic," schizophrenic, holding no true meaning.[x] With the same experiential ethos, a few hundred kilometers south of Zürich, Hungarian dance artist Rudolf von Laban operated a school on Monté Verità, a hill outside the town of Ascona. A utopian colony attracting a wide range of artists, thinkers, spiritualists, nudists, and writers of the day (a guest list that included both Weber and Jung), it was a diverse mix of energies, eccentrics and organizations often in direct conflict with each other's ideas, but united implicitly in their emphasis on self-experimentation and the search for new forms of enchantment. What they shared in common was an idea Jung himself had expressed: cultural change must first go through liberation of the individual.

Jung's views about religion and spirituality were clearly shaped by his profession as a psychiatrist as well as his scientific persona, which stressed careful empirical observation. The religious was for him first and foremost an individual experience, one that had little to do with the dogmas and creeds he saw the church imposing on it. Religion, for Jung, was above all an attitude of psychological exploration of what Rudolf Otto aptly termed the *numinosum*. Jung's writing explains:

> Religion appears to me to be a peculiar attitude of mind which could be formulated in accordance with the original use of the word *religio*, which means a careful consideration and observation of certain dynamic factors that are conceived as "powers": spirits, daemons, gods, laws, ideas, ideals, or whatever name man has given to such factors in his world as he has found powerful, dangerous, or helpful enough to be devoutly worshipped and loved.[xi]

Jung further defined the *numinosum* as a "dynamic agency or effect not caused by an arbitrary act of will."[xii] Following this definition, a religious person is an individual with a particular attitude "peculiar to a consciousness which has been changed by experience of the *numinosum*."[xiii] This was the attitude change he himself had gone through after his break with Freud and his own turn inward to psyche, an experience that enabled him, in a TV interview, to answer the question of whether or not he believed in God with, "I don't need to believe, I know."[xiv]

Jung's understanding of religion's emergence from personal experience of the *numinosum* gives us the essential background for better understanding the particular school of psychoanalysis his followers formed during the first decades of the twentieth century. In a letter to P.W. Martin, Jung wrote: "You are quite right, the main interest of my work is not concerned with the treatment of neuroses but rather with the approach to the numinous."[xv] It was within the spiritual experiences of each individual that a "cure" was to be found. Jung declared that the "escape from the state of reduction lies in evolving a religion of an individual character,"[xvi] a clear counterposition to the established religions of the time. Techniques such as "active imagination," personal analysis, and in-depth comparative studies of mythology and folklore were seen as a means of reconnecting with the "collective unconscious," our cultural heritage mediated through its often numinous and healing archetypal images.

Throughout the process he later named "individuation," a certain change of attitude was to be observed in the individual: a personal transformation involving a shift in personality in which the ego takes second position to what Jung called the Self. Jung wrote about the Self that it "might equally well be called the 'God within us.'"[xvii] The aim of this often lifelong process of individuation is not to become perfect, but "whole." This was the "constructive method" Jung would spend the rest of his life, if not perfecting, so deepening. In it was an alluring message of personal re-enchantment that would be welcomed by the spiritually depleted society that had just been drawn into yet another horrific world war. It was a spiritual seed that would grow roots in the liberal soil of the American continent but that would grow into something quite different than Jung perhaps had imagined.

Jung, Gross, and the coming of a new age

The horrors revealed after the end of World War II and the fall of the German National Socialist regime showed once again the devastating effects of humanity's technological advances. The nuclear bombs over Nagasaki and Hiroshima and the images of ruined European cities left the post-war human with less trust in himself and society. Stability and safety were what the collective craved. The fast-growing post-war marketplace was eager to transform the wartime economy into something more peaceful by promising stability while channeling excessive libido into consumption. New automobile models, household products, instant coffee brands, and deodorants were advertised as part of an idealized American lifestyle. The new mass medium of television exported the same internationally, interspersed with the emerging popular culture of soap operas and rock music. Had the pioneering spiritual lust of Jung and his like been smothered by the 1950s' search for stability?

No, behind the conservative facade of conspicuous consumption and ad images of idealized lifestyles, new ideas and values were cooking collectively. A new generation started to make themselves heard and would soon begin to question the American dream as promoted by the "Hidden Persuaders" of Madison Avenue. Ironically later labelled the "Pepsi Generation," this was a generation grown up on television, hamburgers, and popular culture—one that would question the authenticity of the freedom promoted by the establishment. A new type of individual was taking shape—eager to break with parents' traditions, values, and beliefs—in a countercultural revolution that would turn to Jung's methods of inward-looking self-realization and personal transformation as a means to political freedom. It was to be spiced up with a sexual ingredient supplied by Jung's "twin brother," Otto Gross.

"... [I]n Gross I discovered many aspects of my

own nature, so that he often seemed like my twin brother—but for the Dementia praecox,"[xviii] Jung wrote Freud in one of his letters in 1908. Jung seems to have had an ambivalent relation to Gross from their first meeting. Gross had been sent to Jung by Freud for personal analysis. After one week of intensive therapy, Jung wrote back to him saying that "[h]e [Gross] is an extraordinarily decent fellow with whom you can hit it off at once provided you can get your own complexes out of the way."[xix] Later, Jung admitted to being inspired by him when developing his concept of the introverted and extraverted personality types (which Gross had labelled "restricted but deep consciousness" and "wide but superficial" consciousness respectively). As time went by, though, he would largely dismiss Gross' contribution to psychology and describe him as somewhat of a tragic figure who "... hung out with artists, writers, political dreamers and degenerates of any description, and in the swamps of Ascona... celebrated miserable and cruel orgies."[xx] It has been speculated that the reason for Jung's negative attitude was that his own analysis with Gross surfaced split sides in his personality that were too difficult to integrate.[xxi]

Regardless, Gross, as an outspoken anarchist, was much more politically radical than both Jung and Freud. Like Jung, he saw that collective change had to happen within the individual:

challenging the authorities of society had to begin by confronting the inner authority or father figure within our own psyche. In contrast to Jung, Gross also stated that no real change could take place in the individual if society did not change first. To this politicization of psychoanalytic ideas he added a sexual component, one that stood in sharp contrast to Freud's theory of libido. Where Freud saw the importance of using the analytic technique in helping individuals to strengthen their ego defenses in order to better protect themselves (and society) from the "*Id*," the individual's instinctual animal nature run wild, Gross argued the opposite, that it is the repression of instinct that causes neurosis in the modern human. Gross was the first to propose a "sexual revolution" and liberation of the libidinal energy of humankind. In this way he saw that society could be liberated and free its individuals from repressive authorities. For Gross, psychoanalysis was not a bourgeois luxury for a wealthy few but "a weapon in a countercultural revolution to overthrow the existing order."[xxii]

It was Gross' anarchistic take on Freud's psychoanalytical ideas, coupled with Jung's spiritual method, that would help form parts of the psychological backdrop of the countercultural movement taking form on the American west coast in the mid-1960s, a political uprising that would come to realize Gross' vision of sexual liberation and initiate international anti-Vietnam-War demonstrations. Jung and Gross would influence the movement with a spiritual and political inspiration often attributed to other more public thinkers such as Herbert Marcuse of the Frankfurt School and Wilhelm Reich, another of Freud's rejected disciples. The collective was rising up— the personal had become political and was eager to realize political liberation through personal transformation.

Monté Verità goes global

John F. Kennedy, 1963; Malcolm X, 1965; Martin Luther King, 1968: the counterculture and its hope for political change through personal liberation faded as quickly as it had arisen, as each of its icons of freedom were shot down one after another. In the 1970s, the Vietnam War continued to rage; oil prices surged; and the economy recessed. Instead of turning to politics, more people in the counterculture would escape within themselves through a new means of self-realization that had started to flood the market under the umbrella of the "New Age." It was Monté Verità gone global in a fast-growing consumerist market driven by a thirst for personal liberation. The "human potential movement," Eastern philosophy, and yoga practices were competing with primal scream therapy, self-psychology, EST, and LSD. An anything-goes philosophy turned the search for political liberation into a search for personalized "peak experiences." The radical political potential of the counterculture was fading. The first part, "changing yourself," had seemed relatively easy. Changing society proved to be more difficult. Social change required patience, consistency, organization, and a strong political basis.

Jung's ideas, however, continued to inspire the growing New Age generation of spiritual seekers. By the mid- and late-1970s, he had risen to posthumous public stardom—outside the world of psychology, largely with the help of Joseph Campbell's release of *The Hero with a Thousand Faces* and the later TV program *The Power of Myth*. Jung's message of self-realization, wholeness, and personal transcendence remained intact, but his methods would be broadly interpreted insofar as his ideas took root in the positivistic, individualized, commercialized culture then thriving on the American continent. In place of the humbly sincere religious attitude of "serving Self" proposed by Jung, a warped and magical attitude was emerging.

The renowned anthropologist Bronisław Malinowski writes about magic that its function is to ritualize humanity's optimism and enhance its faith in the victory of hope over fear.[xxiii] The optimistic and opportunistic attitude that better characterized American culture than it did European would have a significant impact on how Jung's psychology was received and interpreted in America. David Tacey clarifies the links and differences between Jung and the New Age in his article "Jung and the New Age: A Study in Contrasts." He argues that the New Age movement was deeply inspired by Jung, but lost its political and spiritual components in the positivistic, capitalistic soil of America in the 1970s and '80s: "It aims to bring new enchantment and mystery into a world that has grown tired, depressed, and disenchanted."[xxiv]

What is it we see happening to Jung's spiritual method as it meets the American New Age market? A religious attitude turning to magic to serve the purposes of ego? Self taking backseat to ego in an increasingly individualized search for self-realization and differentiation on the marketplace? It is the growth of a consumer culture supporting what seems a rather infantile and narcissistic type of "wholeness" quite different from the one envisioned by Jung—a wholeness that seems more closely related to Freud's description of an "oceanic feeling" governed not by the archetype of the Self but by infantile needs. Inspired by the New Age, a new consumer attitude is born, one in constant need of numinous experiences and endless psychic growth—a magical one, nourished by the marketplace.

Enchanted consumerism

To understand how our modern-day market birthed today's narcissistic consumer, we have to rewind the tape back quickly to the 1960s, when the counterculture first took the corporations by surprise. Initially, the market feared that the new values and lifestyles embraced by this new (Pepsi) generation would threaten the capitalistic engine's relentless need for growth. But as the (market) story so often goes, the problem was handily turned into an opportunity, the solution to be found in "turning to psyche." For Jung, we live in a world of psychic images: "Far from being a material world, this is a psychic world, which allows us to make only indirect and hypothetical inferences about the real nature of matter."[xxv] It was this psychological insight—that we experience our world through psychic images—that would help inspire today's culture of enchanted consumerism. It was to be the image, not the product—the desires, not the needs—that would characterize the modern market's offerings. A market transformation had begun, one that would turn ever more products into enchanted objects of desire appealing to the New-Age-schooled consumer's restless search for self-realization.

To fully understand how this psychic economy feeds on the contemporary consumer, we must

offered on the marketplace as pseudo-substitutes, preserving the expectancy. It is a magical ritual of consumption resulting in what Jung defined as a type of possession and enlargement of personality: "The enlargement may be effected through an accretion from without, by new vital contents finding their way into the personality from outside and being assimilated."[xxx] He follows with the warning that "the more assiduously we follow this recipe, and the more stubbornly we believe that all increase has to come from without, the greater becomes our inner poverty."[xxxi]

Could it be that in our search for personal growth and self-realization, we are simultaneously emptying ourselves and continuously outsourcing more of our desire, psyche, and soul to the market? Is what we have tried to depict here—an enchanted ecosystem of magical rituals—driving today's psychic growth economy? Are we a consumer society made up of psychological surplus dressed in pseudo-spiritual clothing? If so, what we are left with is "human product" incestuously bound to the marketplace, repetitively compelled to feed an empty but constantly hungry branded self.

Technological transcendence

We have travelled quickly through the century in

trying to sketch an alternative narrative of a re-enchanted world characterized by the pseudo-spirituality of the marketplace. Munich, Monté Verità, Jung, Gross, and Dichter; counterculture, New Age, and magical consumerism. Still we have one more stop we need to make briefly in order to complete our speculations: technology. Counterculture turned New Age turned consumer culture would leave more and more people in the collective running themselves ragged in search of "personal growth." There seemed to be a wish to climb one step higher in Abraham Maslow's "hierarchy of needs,"[xxxii] to experience the pinnacle of Jung's own heroic odyssey into the unconscious: transcendence. In the 1980s and 1990s, the market had perfected its methods of brand creation, could easily mirror consumers' inner needs for self-realization. Still, it struggled to sell wholeness and transcendence.

It was with the new technology of the personal computer and the coming of the Internet that the opportunity would present itself. Jung wrote that the archetype of the "Self" and wholeness hides behind the mask of technique. "It is characteristic of our time that the archetype, in contrast to its previous manifestations, should now take the form of an object, a technological construction, in order to avoid the odiousness of mythological personification. Anything that looks technological goes down without difficulty with modern man."[xxxiii] How were computer and communications technologies in the hands of the market to be transformed into a promise of personal transcendence?

Back in the early '70s, as the counterculture and New Age movements were still busy confronting inner and outer authorities, and the marketers were experimenting with new ways of injecting desire into more and more products, on the American west coast, another movement was ripening. In *What the Dormouse Said: How the '60s Counterculture Shaped the Personal Computer Industry*, John Markoff recounts how a new generation of computer hackers and programmers was heavily influenced by the countercultural ethos in building what would become the personal computer (PC).[xxxiv] It was a new generation of inventers and entrepreneurs planting the seeds of what would become Silicon Valley that saw computers not merely as technical tools but as a means of expanding the human mind, as "extensions of the self." The hub of this activity was Stanford University and its two laboratories, the Stanford Artificial Intelligence Laboratory and the Augmented Human Intellect Research Center. The latter was built around a vision of computing's capacity to help augment the human mind. Many of the technologies first developed by this generation of pioneers would, in the late 1970s and early '80s, inspire the two Steves (Steve Jobs and Steve

Wozniak), busy in a garage in Palo Alto, California, creating the first Apple computer—a computer that would in turn inspire Microsoft to develop the PC, a tool that would change the lives of millions and dramatically influence how we live our lives today.

Marshall McLuhan explains in his seminal book *Understanding Media* the link between the human being and technology: "... [O]ur human senses, of which all media are extensions, are also fixed charges on our personal energies, and... configure the awareness and experience of each one of us."xxxv He ends his introductory chapter by quoting Jung's discussion of the role of slaves in the Roman Empire, wherein Jung claims that every Roman in that society was inwardly a slave: "... [L]iving constantly in the atmosphere of slaves, he became infected through the unconscious with their psychology. No one can shield himself from such an influence."xxxvi McLuhan, through Jung, helps us make the point that people today become like and start to think like the media and computer technologies they consume.

Following this thinking, it becomes clearer that today's communication technology constitutes a psychic extension of the self, an extension onto which the human being seems to project her religious drive and search for transcendence. The ubiquity of computers, networks, email, and the worldwide web seems in this light to carry an implicit promise of transcendence of our psychic as well as physical limitations as humans. As computers today become personal parts of every person's home, shrunken into pocket-sized mobile phones, and wirelessly connected to the Internet, we are for brief moments allowed, magically, to transcend mundane reality. We are welcomed into a virtual network of constant entertainment, information, and communication. Together with this transformation comes the promise of ubiquitous godlike lifestyles characterized by limitless economic and psychic growth and enabled by the outsourcing of parts of our psyche (memory, images, text, music, friends) to communications technologies.

This final digression on technology serves the purpose of this chapter in providing another clue to where people's need for the numinous is being projected today. The world has indeed been undergoing a steady process of re-enchantment. Simply stated, the consumption of computer technology is another example of a pseudo-spiritual practice in our twenty-first-century marketplace, one carrying the enchanted hope of transcending life's limitations on earth—when in reality we are transcending into a state of "*participation mystique*" with the machines, hardly reflecting on what parts of our humanity we are giving up.

Brandpsycho

2

THE BRAND COMPLEX

"If the development of civilization has such a far-reaching similarity to the development of the individual and if it employs the same methods, may we not be justified in reaching the diagnosis that, under the influence of cultural urges, some civilizations... [and] possibly the whole of mankind have become 'neurotic.'"

– Sigmund Freud, *Civilization and Its Discontents* [xxxvii]

In order to make sense of the hypothesis presented in this chapter, that brands are structured like psychological complexes and can have pathological effects on culture and therefore the human psyche, we need first to understand "complex theory" a bit better in the context of the psychoanalytical school of Carl Gustav Jung.

In 1902, when Jung was working at the Burghölzli psychiatric clinic in Zürich, he began conducting experiments using his "word association test." He wanted to understand how the mind works beyond the limits of consciousness. He worked with a list of words he would read in turn to each participant, who would respond to each word spontaneously with the first word that came to mind. Jung would note participants' responses, reaction times, emotional expressions, and defensive attitudes. He noticed that certain words triggered in participants emotional reactions that interrupted their conscious thought processes. He saw these disturbances as indicative of the existence of unconscious "complexes."

Jung's word association experiment led him to theorize that there are unconscious structures below the surface of human consciousness—that the building blocks of the psyche are made up of a person's repressed memories, fantasies, ideas, and images. Jung would later refer to this collection of repressed content as the personal unconscious. He observed that, "[w]hen stimulated, this network of associated material... produces a disturbance in consciousness."[xxxviii] Constellating a complex is like pressing a button: an automatic reaction starts, and the person is no longer in conscious control of his actions, but caught in his complex.[xxxix] This is an insight bound to animate not only the field of psychology but also the study of persuasion.

Later on in his career, Jung would argue that behind every complex is an archetypal image, an organizing pattern rooted in the deepest strata of the psyche's "collective unconscious." The collective unconscious, he explained, is humanity's psychic heritage, an impersonal reservoir of our species' instincts. One could describe the archetype and the instinct as two sides of the same coin, the archetype being the form the instincts assume. Archetypes, for Jung, are not only constellated within the psyche of the individual, but make themselves present in the collective through the process of unconscious projection.[xl] By studying the stories and myths that make up the world we live in, therefore, we can learn to recognize repeated collective fantasies functioning in the world as powerful psychic forces influencing cultural change.

Extending Jung's complex theory and treatment of archetypes beyond the clinic and into cultural analysis demands careful consideration of the complexity inherent in all collective change processes. A psychological interpretation needs to be undertaken hermeneutically, drawing on analyses of relevant historical, political, social, and economic discourses, and relating each part of the analysis to the whole in order not to simplify the complexity of the studied phenomena. That said, psychoanalysis and complex theory, when used correctly, can be useful tools in revealing the irrational motivations that underlie cultural conflict, an emphasis often lacking in the dominant sociological, political, and economic approaches with which we are most familiar.

The what, why, and how of branding

Say the word *brand* and many associate it with the logotype of a given multinational corporation—or with advertising in general, the conspicuous marketing of consumer goods—something of relatively little importance in our lives. The reality is different: brands and the discourse of branding affect everyone living in consumer societies. Brands reflect aspects of the collective fantasies of our culture. They are valuable objects of investigation in culture studies because they contain veiled information about culture's *zeitgeist* and dominant ideas and ideals. Indeed, the branding process may be thought of as the psychological engine powering the marketplace today.

Etymologically, *brand* derives from Old Norse, a Viking language spoken in Scandinavia until the fourteenth century. *Brandr* meant "to burn."[xli] Later in history, the word came to identify the process of marking things—cattle, criminals, or slaves, for example—with a hot iron. Today, branding is still about burning, but now we the consumers are the cattle, and the marks are sustained psychologically. Brands today are created not in the world of matter but in the minds of people.

Psychoanalytically speaking, a brand is an *imago*, a representative psychological entity comprised of the meanings, images, and fantasies associated with a given product, person, or experience. But to give credit to those who still equate a brand with its logotype, it all started there. Branding has gone through a process of development in its over-a-century-long service to our economy, and can be divided into three phases or eras: *logos*, *eros*, and *mythos.*

The brand took its first stumbling steps in the Americas of the mid-nineteenth century, a time when people still defined who they were by what they produced, not what they consumed. At that time, a brand was just as simple as its logotype. The role it played in the economy was that of a signifier of quality: it differentiated a product from those belonging to a company's competitors and "burned" the company name onto that company's own products. Products in the era of *logos* had no real identity because consumption was still mainly about needs, not desires.

Branding's adolescent years, the era of *eros*, started in the middle of the 1950s alongside the shift away from a traditional society of producers to the modern consumer era wherein advertising itself became more image- than text-based. The consumption myth that we are still being asked to believe today—that supply is being driven by consumer demand, that the market produces what consumers want—is false. Supply in fact outgrew demand sometime after the Second World War, prompting an extreme economic makeover that transformed faceless products into brands, and a society of producers into consumers.

The word *consume* traces its etymological roots to fifteenth-century French in the word *consumere,* "to use up, eat, waste." A consumer was seen as someone "who squanders or wastes" or has committed an "act of pillage, looting, or plundering." Overall, the word has quite a negative connotation (the old word for tuberculosis was *consumption*).[xlii] In a 1955 article, economist Victor Lebow described the kind of transformation he thought the economy would need to undergo if the market's demand for constant growth was to be met: "Our enormously productive economy demands that we make consumption our way of life, that we convert the buying and use of goods into rituals, that we seek our spiritual satisfactions, our ego satisfactions in consumption... We need things consumed, burned up, worn out, replaced, and discarded at an ever increasing rate."[xliii] The success of the emerging consumer economy would lie not in its products but in how effectively it could endow consumers with a set of economically useful psychological attributes. The branded self was born.[xliv]

Advertising in this era of *eros* did not so much stress a product's features as emphasize the emotional gratification a product could offer (three marketing favorites even today include joy, health, and security) through the use of imagery and sensory appeal and by stimulating our unconscious, often hidden, desires. Psychoanalytic theory had taught companies that people are not only rational but also irrational about their choices, motivated by unconscious desire for pleasure and satisfaction—the *raison d'être* of which desire "is not to realize its goal, to find full satisfaction, but to reproduce itself as desire."[xlv] Companies at this time started investing more money in the design of a brand image (*imago*) for their products: "role-model identities" representing what people longed for and sometimes felt lacking in themselves were now available on the market for a price.

Since then, brands, branding, and society at large have moved on to the current postmodern paradigm, what sociologist Zygmunt Bauman refers to as an individualized, globalized "liquid modernity"[xlvi] of digital communications in a secular context of gradually deconstructing identities and traditions. For Bauman, postmodern identity is constructed individually, in a continuously reflexive and dynamic way, in relation to the environment. Never fixed—it is always changing. The life project of the secularized citizen is the therapeutic project of selfhood—the constant search for peak experiences—a life in dyadic relationship to the marketplace in the formation of a branded self. Our constant consumption of the images and ideals sold on the marketplace helps us form a sense of identity.

The role of brands in this new world of *mythos* is therefore no longer simply to infuse goods with desire, but rather to help construct the narratives, stories, mythologies, and lifestyles that people seek in order to control and create meaning in their lives. Commercial brands have become pieces in the therapeutic puzzle that is postmodern identity: today we consume through products and services what we search for and lack in ourselves.

Over the course of this historical development, "*logos-eros-mythos*," the role of brands has evolved from helping people identify products, to helping products stand out appealingly on the market, to assisting consumers in identifying ourselves— who we are and what makes us different from each other. Tightly compressed, this is the what, why, and how of branding. We now have enough context to begin our analysis of brands as complexes and to demonstrate the hypothesis that today's postmodern immersion in *mythos* might not lead to brand utopia, but rather to a contemporary consumer complex, a brand neurosis.

Analysis: Brands as complexes

The argument for brands being constructed like complexes is built on five observations made in light of a comparative study of two fields: analytical psychology (specifically "complex theory") and branding. The observations are as follows:

1. Brands as well as complexes are constructed psychic realities built on personal experiences.
2. Their "glue" is emotion.
3. They may disturb and override conscious thinking.
4. Collectively constellated, they can unite people around a common purpose.
5. When powerful, they often connect to an archetypal core.

Let's have a more detailed look at each of these observations.

1. Complexes/brands are constructed psychic realities

While Freud's view was that most of human instinct could be reduced to the sexual drive and pleasure-seeking life force of desire or libido, Jung equated the latter with psychic energy. In Jung's investigation of complexes, he saw that there were also other drives (such as hunger, safety, power, creativity, spirituality) that motivate human action. He saw that libido first seeks the mother's body, "but when libido finds a spiritual idea or image it will go there."[xlvii] The key insight that marketers picked up on here was that products could be reconstructed into symbols and analogs that mirror, direct, carry, or bind our libidinal and psychic energy (of which money is another symbol).

Viewed this way, brands are carefully constructed symbols aimed at triggering individuals' emotional reactions by offering imaginative solutions to instinctual drives. Just like complexes, they are psychic-energy constructions formed out of experiences—not traumatic ones from childhood, but based on repeated contact with advertising and other marketing communications.

2. The "glue" behind a complex/brand is emotion

The glue behind the images that a stimulated complex activates is often made up of strong repressed emotions. What makes a brand a brand

48

and a complex a complex is, in each case, its deep emotional resonance for the individual. Mainstream brand-building practice is a structured process of defining the "core identity" and "brand personality" of a product[xlviii]—a process that involves strategically injecting goods with "*pneuma*," spirit, and desire—and charging the product with the emotions and associations that best reflect the desires of the target group (discovered beforehand in focus groups or through consumer research, another psychoanalytic inspiration). The brand personality is thereafter activated through package design, advertising, and popular culture endorsements, and positioned within the cultural discourse of the target group to enhance emotional identification, initiating a projection dance between individuals' desires and the emotional offering of the product.

3. Complexes/brands override conscious thinking

Through his word association experiment, Jung learned that complexes interfere with the will's intentions and disturb consciousness. In Jung's description, complexes behave like independent beings, disrupting the ego with affect and influencing actions as though by "pushing a button." Since consumer society's earliest days, the search for the purchase button has been the holy quest for marketers. Already in 1960, psychoanalyst and motivational researcher Ernest Dichter understood that there are contexts in which emotions such as love, hate, or jealousy will override consumers' economic decision rules based on deductive reasoning.[xlix] *Logos* calls for rational thinking, prompting a conscious decision-making process. *Eros* stimulates fantasies, stirring emotions and images that often override reason and lead to action. Which would you choose if you were the marketer?

4. Collectively constellated complexes/brands unite people

According to Jungian analyst Thomas Singer, "Intense collective emotion is the hallmark of an activated cultural complex... Cultural complexes structure emotional experience... [They] can provide those caught in their potent web of stories and emotions a simplistic certainty about the group's place in the world."[l] Since the 1980s, consumer marketing has been focused on creating "lifestyles" for consumers in which goods help shape the pattern of one's life, in which values, ideas, and identity are co-created together with brands. Since the middle of the 1990s and the explosion of the Internet, the focus has increasingly shifted to creating "tribes" and "brand communities" who share similar experiences and emotions[li] and are defined as non-geographical communities "based on a set of structured relations between admirers of a brand... [such as] shared consciousness, rituals and traditions and a sense of moral responsibility... [and] a sense of... being different from other people."[lii] Psychoanalytically speaking, the focus of today's marketing lies in constructing collective consumer cultural complexes that unite people around a brand. While we are at it, are you an Apple or a PC?

5. Complexes/brands connect to an archetypal core

A brand, much like a complex (in Jung's description), is a nucleus with two parts: an emotional part rooted in the personal unconscious, and an archetypal part, the primitive core and organizing principle of which resides in the deepest strata of the collective unconscious. Instinctual by nature, we can only obtain access to archetypes through their images. These archetypal images are not and cannot be constructed, but according to Jung they make up the building blocks of the human psyche and human existence. In the paradigm of *mythos*, and as brands take on more human attributes, become personalities, and no longer function simply to help identify a product but to help consumers identify themselves, brands turn from logotypes to the archetypes.

Archetypes, not logotypes, are at the core of the brand-building process today, and by consciously and unconsciously coupling with their positive attributes, a company weaves its identity, communications, and personality around them. What is hoped for is an instinctual identification with the consumer on an archetypal level, a feat achieved by associating with the attributes of the archetype with which consumers most likely want to identify but perhaps cannot manage in reality.

Three examples may be usefully studied in this context. I have undertaken two of these studies (Apple and Starbucks) in the next two chapters.

1. Sports giant Nike capitalizes on the archetype of the Warrior, using battle imagery in their overall communications to offer to their customers a sense of mastery.
2. Apple Inc. associates with the archetype of the Magi-cian and promises transcendence through technology and empowerment of the individual.[liii]
3. Starbucks Coffee makes use of the archetype of the Great Mother in embedding customers in a multi-sensorial experience

and connecting them to a deep sense of longing for community and home.

A constructed unconsciousness?

Do these observations convince us that brands are a kind of complex? Some would argue that they are not because they are not inside of us but in the external world. But wait a minute: inside of us is *exactly* where they are. Brands are constructed consciously in the external world but are activated within individual psyches through the process of projection. Perhaps a better way to put this would be to say that brands are constructed to function as, and to activate, complexes (keeping in mind that Jung said that a complex does not have to be negative in itself, but that its consequences often are).

This meta-discussion of external and internal, object and subject, leads to the question of what constitutes psychic reality. Jung, in the tradition of Descartes, Locke, and Kant, makes a distinction between the living subjective world of psyche and the material world of dead matter—a dualistic view of a world with a distinct border that can only be crossed in the subjective process of imaginative projection. James Hillman, founder of the school of Archetypal Psychology and a follower of Jung, claims differently. He argues that the catastrophic situation of the world today, with its natural disasters, famines, and hyper-capitalistic excesses, calls for this duality to be reworked. "For all the while that psychotherapy has succeeded in raising the consciousness of human subjectivity, the world in which all subjectivities are set has fallen apart."[liv] He argues that after psychotherapy's initial focus on the individual psyche in the early twentieth century, it moved on to focus instead on the relationships between people (e.g. object relations, self-psychology); today it has a new role to play in healing the bleeding wound that makes up the split between the object and subject world. Psychoanalysis viewed in this way is not something that happens only in the analytical room between two people, but also on the streets, in our relation to the environment and objects around us.

Hillman proposes that we pick up where Freud left off and begin to examine our own culture with "a pathological eye"—a return to Plato's *"Anima Mundi"* and a reality in which all life is enchanted, in which we see the soul-spark of life in spirit and matter. "The *anima mundi* indicates the animated possibilities presented by each event as it is... its availability to imagination, its presence as a *psychic* reality."[lv] Going back to go forward again, we imagine a world that gives reality to psyche as something that exists within itself, independently of the subject, "ensouled" in the material of external reality.

I am digressing, but it is worth speculating whether Hillman's animistic vision of reality may have been adopted, in a twisted way, by today's companies in the branded era of *mythos*. We have learned that branding can be seen as a strategic process of giving life, identity, and meaning to a dead commodity—the commercial process of transforming objects into subjects, making them alive with ever more human attributes constructed on the "*prima materia*" of emotion, complexes, and archetypes.

No, I am not saying that branding represents a renaissance of the *Anima Mundi*, but the contrary. A phantasmagoria, perhaps? Perhaps our culture's one-sided focus on economic growth makes us vulnerable to a powerful craving for emotional identification. And the fantasies sold by brands have been all too ready to oblige.

Let us change lenses so that we can zoom out again. In this new perspective, we can see how the practice of branding unveils something that looks like a new field of consciousness in our external reality. A "constructed unconscious," that is, a psychologically mediated reality made up of a plethora of intentionally constructed images, myths, complexes, and desires—unconscious for the majority of us—contains, or seems to contain, everything we search for and dream about, repackaged and sold back to us by marketers. A fog (smog?) seems to settle over reality, which, in the name of neverending growth, serves our desires and forms something we might think of as a contemporary consumer complex.

The symptoms

When taking on the endeavor of labelling neurotic an entire collective, it makes sense first to carefully scrutinize one's own underlying motivations and potential neuroses. "I am not in the least neurotic—touch wood!",[lvi] wrote Jung in his last personal correspondence to Freud before they separated, mainly due to their differences of opinion on the origin of neurosis. Where Freud saw unresolved infantile sexual fantasies rooted in early childhood as the cause of neuroses later in life, Jung sought answers in the present. Jung's investigations were not necessarily limited to repressed sexuality, but were often based on more existential matters, namely the challenges of living a meaningful life.

As we saw in the previous chapter, Jung viewed neurosis as a symptom of maladjustment, disunity with oneself—a dissociation activated by the complexes, but also an attempt at self-cure and self-healing. Keeping these characteristics in mind, let us take a closer look at the symptoms of the neurosis demonstrated by contemporary consumer culture.

"Breakdown extends to every component of civic life because civic life is now a constructed life,"[lvii] says Hillman, and it seems true that the constructed unconscious fantasies molded by the branding paradigm have played a great part in this development. But now it is time to get more specific.

As in all analyses, we start by examining the symptoms of our patient carefully, one by one, before closing the hermeneutical circle and putting the pieces together into a whole. The most revealing symptoms of the neurosis our contemporary consumer culture exhibits are as follows: fragmentation, dissociation, and cognitive dissonance. In the machine that is the branding train, we may discover dynamics actively contributing to and belligerently continuing to feed collective brand neurosis. Let us examine each symptom individually.

Fragmentation

Continual exposure to unresolved complexes causes an individual's ego to dissolve slowly in strength, leaving the neurotic patient with a sense of falling apart, a fragmented disintegrated state of consciousness that instigates anxiety. Branding is a structured process of constructing, mirroring, and thereby accentuating complexes in individuals within a collective. Unlike earlier power techniques, branding thrives on differences and heterogeneity.

To consume brands means to introduce a difference into one's life—to be different (or, as in the case of Apple, to "Think Different").

The "liquid identity" of the postmodern consumer exhibits many of the attributes apparent in a fragmented psyche. Never fixed, always changing, in a liminal state between being and wanting, he is caught in a neurotic tension of relentless, always-unsatisfied desire. It is an uncomfortable state for the individual, but a profitable one for the market. The postmodern psyche wishes at any price to escape this feeling of disintegration, constantly searching for a sense of identity, belonging, mastery, and selfhood. We find, in consequence, an endless narcissistic preoccupation with social identity and self, unconsciously projected onto the reflexive meeting with "the Other": brands, social media, and communications technologies. Constructing identity through narratives of experience and consumption, by identifying with the social mask of our persona, we form a branded self.

In the process of globalization, as traditional institutions, religions, and authorities lose more of their power, the marketplace takes on a therapeutic role: "... economic entities (and mostly brands) have taken the symbolic place left empty by the retreat of the divine."[lviii] To escape this fragmentation, people anxiously search for a sense of community and belonging. Adapting to a certain lifestyle, building an identity within a brand community, and becoming part of a "tribe" may temporarily relieve such tensions. Holding hands over national borders, we are united by our brand complexes and belief in consumption and the free-market utopia.

Dissociation

"If one is to rule, and to continue ruling, one must be able to dislocate the sense of reality,"[lix] wrote George Orwell in his book *1984*. Dissociation is "a partial or complete disruption of the normal integration of a person's psychological functioning."[lx] In the last half-century, brands seem to have been cautiously constructed to lead our libido astray by stimulating and mirroring our unconscious complexes and instinctual desires. Having been sold an image of reality, a product's *imago*, we are promised emotional gratification that is never satisfied other than illusorily.

Branding seems to be intent on altering the state of reality, advocating delusion through fantasy, stirring up desires, and stimulating complexes. Branding seems to have fostered a culture of irrationality in which the answers to our most precious and intimate needs for love, meaning, and identity have become projected and mediated through brands. Consumers are kept running on the spot, on the spinning wheel of desire—what Schopenhauer referred to as the "wheel of Ixion"— endlessly pursuing new desires. The effect of this is what French philosopher Jean Baudrillard described as "hyperreality," where the sign, image, and symbol become more real than reality.[lxi]

Cognitive dissonance

Brands are self-contradictory by nature. On the one hand they offer a road to paradise, Utopia ("a sort of absent presence, an unreal reality, a kind of nostalgic elsewhere"),[lxii] by promoting the emancipatory values of freedom, self-expression, and liberation (*eros* and *mythos*). On the other hand they are practical (*logos*) if not banal. Their offering has to be partly practical, reasonable, and readily comparable to other products in the same product category in order to generate brand loyalty and repeated purchases. Always promising a better tomorrow and the chance of improvement, but only by taking action now, again and again: a new and improved product must always replace the old and obsolete one.

This inner contradiction of brands has been likened to George Orwell's definition of "doublethink": "... [t]he power of holding two contradictory beliefs in one's mind simultaneously, and accepting both of them."[lxiii] Doublethink means "to hold simultaneously two opinions which cancelled out... [C]onsciously to induce unconsciousness, and then, once again, to become unconscious of the act of hypnosis you had just performed."[lxiv] The paradoxical nature of brands, their simultaneous contradictory offerings, stimulates in the collective what in psychological terms is referred to as "cognitive distortion." Designating exaggerated and irrational thoughts,[lxv] it is a term often used together with "cognitive dissonance," a discomfort caused by holding conflicting ideas simultaneously[lxvi]—in other words, as we have already seen, doublethink.

The theory of cognitive dissonance was originally introduced by social psychologist Leon Festinger in his classic 1956 book *When Prophecy Fails*.[lxvii] The research material for Festinger's book was taken from a field study he did with his colleagues, in which they secretly infiltrated an American UFO cult that had prophesized the end of the world. The team wanted to test Festinger's hypothesis, that the psychological consequences of a group of individuals' disconfirmed expectations could be described as a form of cognitive dissonance. Indeed, when the cult's prophecy failed (as they had quite naturally predicted), Festinger and his colleagues saw their hypothesis confirmed.

Festinger drew the further conclusion that individuals have a "motivational drive" to relieve dissonance, an insight that some cognitive-oriented schools of therapy have picked up on today. But encouraging people to alter their own thoughts and offering cognitive techniques for treating symptoms results in a disturbance in an individual's psyche. It should be quite clear that we, given our theory of brands as constructed complexes communicated and experienced in doublethink, take a radically different stand.

We see that the practice of branding seems to stimulate cognitive dissonance in our consumer culture by repeatedly disconfirming expectations and only offering temporary, imagined gratification in answer to real and very pressing cultural needs. Therefore treatments of such disturbances directed at the individual risk being counterproductive—risk trying to adapt healthy individuals to a culture showing severe signs of neurosis.

Diagnosis: Brand neurosis

It is time for us to close the hermeneutic circle. We have learned that brands can be likened to complexes, constructed fields of psychic energy and emotion irrationally overriding consciousness and, when archetypally linked, uniting people collectively. We have discussed the borders of psychic reality and speculated that branding as a historical process has fashioned a "constructed unconscious" (unconscious for the majority of us), containing what we dream of and search for, repackaged and sold back to us as promises. Standing on firm soil—having scrutinized our own intentions—we felt confident in presenting our hypothesis that built into the process of branding are dynamics that actively contribute to and aggressively continue to feed the construction of a collective consumer complex, a "brand neurosis." This is an assertive claim we have tried to test by carefully inspecting the most observable symptoms our contemporary consumer psyche displays, namely fragmentation, dissociation, and cognitive dissonance.

What we have presented is merely a hypothesis. The symptoms depicted in our analysis are not due only to the process of branding and the influence of brands on consumer culture. No, these are merely partial explanations of the phenomena. Before a more vigorous theory can be presented, further studies—taking into consideration macro factors from the social, economic, and political fields combined—are needed, as is more empirical research and data.

Now, the million dollar question is, what can we do about all of this? We agreed earlier that brands exist in our minds, that they are psychological constructions. Just as church and religion lost power when they lost symbolic significance in people's lives, brands will lose power as more people become aware of their illusory undertakings. A part of this work of awareness is individual and involves separating our own neurosis from that of the collective.

But more importantly, by de:branding—lifting the veil and exposing some of branding's techniques and potentially destructive didactics—we start where all change must begin, with making what is unconscious conscious. Today our consumer culture might be trapped in a brand neurosis, but it would be worse to leave it untreated and let it metastasize, in which case we might stand face to face with a psychosis, an abnormal condition of mind in which an individual or collective loses all contact with reality. Is it not our task to use the tools at our disposal to impede the encroachment of brand psychosis?

3
DID YOU BITE
THE MAGIC APPLE?

Let's be honest: Apple creates excellent products. Without these products, there would be no magic and no brand. But there is more to Apple than the items it sells, and in this chapter we will focus our attention on Apple's cultural significance. What do its products mean at the level of *mythos*? What can we make of the brand's popularity? What are the deeper layers of its symbolism?

When Apple entered the computer market in the late 1970s, it entered a world structurally dominated by masculinity and *logos*. A technocratic, instrumental outlook set the tone for the field, with IBM being exemplary of this attitude. What Apple brought into this cold world of computer technology was *eros*, a more feminine and humanistic approach, together with a vision of democratizing computer technology by making it more accessible to individuals.

The *eros* that Apple embodied reflected the aesthetic, cultural, and spiritual values of Steve Jobs, who was driven by an extraverted intuitiveness and influenced by Zen Buddhism. The philosophy of Zen centers on the search for direct insight into the universe through the long, constant, patient practice of meditation. It emphasizes action over theory, and cultivates a sense of simplicity inspired by its Japanese heritage. With its products, Apple introduced a more intuitive and direct way to engage with and relate to computers by breaking down the traditional borders between human and machine, between subject and object. The introduction of the "mouse" with the first Macintosh computer, for example, opened up a new, more immediate way to relate to the computer screen's graphical interface. Apple's products, then, in their sleekness and simplicity, evoked a Zen sensibility and a beauty that might be considered humanistic.

But this is not all. In order to connect on the deepest levels of participation *mythos*, Apple has (unconsciously and partly consciously) become a symbol for the contemporary collective's search for transcendence through technology (a search previously discussed in our first chapter). Historian David Franklin Noble writes in his book *The*

Religion of Technology that in an attempt to regain a lost sense of divinity, we have come to identify technology with transcendence, approaching it as a gateway to salvation and redemption from the brokenness of the world and humanity's limitations.[lxviii]

In order to understand Apple as a manifestation of Steve Jobs' quest for meaning—a quest on which he was able to connect to changes in the collective unconscious—let us look more closely at how Apple's mythology has helped the brand to become a projection surface for globalized societies' deepest collective desires.

Apple's mythology: The early days

Jungian analyst James Hillman writes that "we emerge into life as creatures in a drama, scripted by the great storytellers of our culture."[lxix] The strength of these dramas, or in another word, myths, is that we live them unconsciously as truths. What is unconscious in people is most often projected outside. In the case of Apple, this projection takes the form of people's belief in the magical quality of the brand's products and stories. "...[M]yth is the natural result of human faith, because every power must give signs of its efficiency, must act and be known to act, if people are to believe in its virtue."[lxx] A great part of Apple's success is related to the way its myths are communicated and how closely they are linked to underlying collective needs. To understand how Apple has achieved such magical qualities, we first have to look back.

"It is now 1984... Will Big Blue dominate the entire computer industry? The entire information age? Was George Orwell right about 1984?"[lxxi] This excerpt is from a keynote speech Steve Jobs gave before showcasing the new Apple television commercial, launched to promote the release of the Macintosh in 1984. The commercial (directed by a young Ridley Scott) takes inspiration from George Orwell's novel *1984*. It shows a female heroine in a white Macintosh-logoed tank top, holding a sledgehammer while running through a dystopian landscape (a cinematic reference to the opening scene of the film classic *Metropolis*). She races toward a large screen bearing the image of a Big-Brother-like Orwellian figure preaching to rows of robotic grey men. She swings the hammer and it crashes into the screen. There is an explosion. The commercial ends with the following lines: "On January 24th, Apple Computer will introduce Macintosh. And you'll see why 1984 won't be like *1984*."[lxxii]

The commercial screened only once, during America's prime-time media mega-occasion, the Super Bowl—a decision further intensifying its mythological proportions. The woman in the commercial clearly personifies the Apple brand, a new liberating *eros* force disrupting the industry's *logos*. A competitive attack on IBM, the ad goes further, symbolically slaying IBM's values while introducing the revolutionary idea of embracing computers as transformative tools that can liberate people from patriarchal authority. Inspired by Jobs' countercultural impetus, a personal computer revolution was born.

Interpreted in this way, the *1984* commercial and Apple's launch of the first Macintosh can be seen as markers of a paradigm shift in collective attitudes. The counterculture hero, an archetypal constellation that had been brewing in the collective since the late 1960s, pregnant in Steve Jobs' psyche, was given new life through Apple. It found its corporate body, entered the market, and spread throughout the world, exporting its associated values to consumers. Apple became an attractor and symbol of this powerful psychic energy. Jobs' sensitivity to this collective shift was his visionary strength. Like the magician who allows lightening to run through him, Jobs can be imagined as having channeled collective energies through his personality and the Apple project. For a long time, Apple's brand mythology would hover around the figure of the countercultural hero.

Apple's myth was heroic and manifested itself

as instinctual drive toward progress and success—a search for identity through mastery of the material, quantifiable, external world. Apple was different from other heroes, though, would come to be seen as a new kind of warrior, one with whom more and more people in the collective could identify. Still, this archetype shared roots with the warrior it was fighting. The need for an ever-present enemy, for a series of challenges to overcome and dragons to slay, is as clear in Jobs' life story as it is in the story of Apple. As is often the case with psychological development, the height of Jobs' success was preceded by a transitional phase.

Transitional phase

Jobs was forced to leave Apple at the age of thirty, an experience that would profoundly change him. During this time, he continued to be successful; he bought and developed the animation graphics company Pixar and founded another computer company called NeXT (later bought by Apple). Jobs described these years as some of the most difficult but also most important in his life. "The heaviness of being successful was replaced by the lightness of being a beginner again, less sure about everything"[lxxiii]—an indirect reference to the

Zen Buddhist concept of looking at the world with a beginner's mind.[lxxiv] This transitional phase in Jobs' life can be viewed in terms of what Joseph Campbell describes as the *initiation* phase of the typical hero's journey, involving separation from the collective, a period of looking inward and questioning old values, and the emergence of new values from the unconscious.[lxxv] Soon Jobs would embark on another heroic quest—by returning to Apple.

A new mythology

In 1997, Apple was a company in crisis, and Jobs' comeback carried the heavy projection of him as its savior. As soon as he returned to the company, Jobs made massive changes, cancelling unprofitable projects and firing staff. In one of his famous keynote speeches, he introduced to the world his re-envisioned Apple. Jobs made it clear that the company's focus would be on Apple's core expertise and on building the brand. He seemed to have understood that the true value the company had developed was not in hardware but in its brand, and that future success depended on having more people believe in its mythology. The launch of this re-envisioned Apple involved retiring the rainbow-striped logo it had used since the '70s, and cultivating a more sophisticated persona.

Jobs' transitional phase and separation from Apple had changed him. He seemed to have left the old warrior attitude behind him—something that became obvious when, to everyone's surprise, he founded a partnership with Microsoft and longtime enemy Bill Gates. Jobs was now back in charge of Apple, poised to fulfill his life quest. True to his characteristic intuitiveness, he was well equipped with new visions and ideas about where he, Apple, and the collective were heading.

A countercultural heroic position could not save Apple from its economic problems. For the collective, this archetype—with its associated attitude of rebellion against authority—seemed to have lost some of its appeal. If we look closely at politically reformative ideas, often we find deeper, sometimes unconscious, spiritual needs buried in their rhetoric. Indeed, some of the spiritual ideas that formed the backdrop of the countercultural liberation movement celebrating the individual's right to self-expression would find their fullest expression in the emerging New Age movement, which was characterized by a lack of organized authority and an emphasis on the individual's transformative potential. It was a spiritual blend of Eastern and ancient wisdom, but it had strong roots in American positivism and individualism.

Self-expression was no longer enough, neither

for Jobs nor Apple, nor for the collective. Behind the emerging desire to be different lay the individual's search for personal transformation—to climb to the highest level of Abraham Maslow's hierarchy of needs—transcendence—and enter a state of being surpassing physical existence that, in one form, is also independent of it. It was a time of growing spiritualism in an age of secularism, and the technical innovations to which it gave rise captured something of its yearning.

Since the 1990s and rise of digital communication, technology has indeed offered virtual transcendence of the limits of our biological existence. Those with Internet access can now connect about anything with anyone at any time. Seen in this way, Apple today offers consumers more than an experience of individuality. The company markets the promise of transformational products and services.[lxxvi] As a brand, Apple is able to take consumers to literal and metaphorical places with the simple touch of a screen. No longer the countercultural hero, Jobs had reinvented himself, and in so doing, shaped a new myth rooted in collective yearning for relationship with the numinous. He had discovered a weapon made of the strongest steel, more powerful than any sword: the archetypal force of magic.

The magic Apple

Anthropologist Bronislaw Malinowski writes that magic differs from religion in that it is purely practical, always performed as a means to an end.[lxxvii] Magic was, in essence, the spiritual ethos of the New Age movement, and yet again Jobs and Apple would manage to capitalize on the shift in collective values it represented, with Apple ultimately becoming a psychic container and symbol for brewing collective needs. The heroic, political, and rebellious attitude of the 1960s and 1970s had warped into the magical, ego-centered attitude of the 1980s and '90s, which focussed on the individual's need for self-transformation and search for transcendence. It is this collective constellation of the archetype of the Magician that we see Apple continuing to capitalize on today. To fully understand how Apple has accomplished this, we turn once more back to Jobs.

The Magician

The archetypical Magician finds opportunities at every turn. The Magician experiences life as a flow of energy, staying open to all possibilities. Steve Jobs seemed to personify and embody the characteristics of this archetype. In interviews with people who worked closely with him, there are frequent references to his "reality distortion field," to how, with a mix of superficial charm, charisma, marketing, appeasement, and persistence, he could prevail. By virtue of his will, he was able to distort his audience's sense of proportion and make them believe a task was possible.[lxxviii] Bill Gates expressed it perhaps most eloquently by saying in a joint interview with Jobs, "The way he does things is just different, and you know, I think it's magical."[lxxix]

The power of magic involves the participation of both the magician and his audience. Jung describes magic as an archetype that always needs the *Ergreifer*, the one who possesses or seizes, as well as the *Ergriffener*, the audience, the one whom the magician possesses. For magic to occur, what is required is "the performing magician quite as much as the thing to be charmed and the means of charming."[lxxx] The magician needs an audience. Magic's powers are not only the magician's; they are the powers of mutuality.

How Jobs the Magician communicated Apple's new myth to its followers becomes most clearly visible in his keynote speeches, which developed over time into evangelical-like gatherings watched by a global audience of millions. Each of them would follow a similar ritual: Jobs would casually walk on stage, praise the new product with enthusiastic superlatives, and the audience would respond with near-deafening applause.

Often repeated in these well-rehearsed presentations were descriptions of Apple's products as magical, awesome, amazing, incredible, and so on. To quote another Apple executive— Rob Johnson, Senior President of Retail—on the occasion of the iPad launch, "This product has to be touched, it has to be held to truly understand how magic it is."[lxxxi] Much as they continue to do today, Apple's products transcended existing product categories. With the introduction of the touch screen, Apple added sensibility, *eros*, and a more intimate way of accessing information: the simple caress of an object of desire.

In the performance of magic, the repetition of a magical spell transforms words into unconsciously accepted truths. And it bears remembering that what a magician "does to a material object will affect equally the person with whom the object was once in contact, whether it formed part of his body or not."[lxxxii] Even after Jobs' death, Apple continues today to cast spells over its audience at the various launches of its new products. Collectively, we remain happily spellbound, and it can rightly be said that the power that pulls us toward these objects is magical.

Conclusion

We are living in a time resembling that of the beginning of the decline of ancient culture and the emergence of Christianity—a time of inner and outer crisis, a time pressing us toward deep-reaching change. The importance of Apple's presence in our lives is due in part to its ability to connect to archetypal changes in the collective unconscious, changes that can be described in terms of the development from the archetypical Warrior to the countercultural Hero, to what we are experiencing today, the Magician.

On the basis of founder Steve Jobs' personality and a well-scripted corporate mythology, Apple has become an icon of worship for a spiritually depleted collective in search of instant meaning and transcendence. Absent the "real thing," magic becomes a substitute for religion, and Apple becomes a vessel containing our collective projections and unconscious longing for identity, divinity, meaning, and technological control.

Apple can be seen as a consumer example of what psychoanalyst Donald Winnicott calls a "transitional object": Apple holds our libido at a time of great change. In the transitional development phase, the one we are in today, both individuals and the collective are seeking secure objects to hold onto, places where we can locate our anxiety. In the case of child development, Winnicott offers teddy bears, dolls, a favorite blanket as examples of transitional objects, that is, physical objects that stand in, from the child's perspective, for the mother-child bond. They are "magical creations, neither all internal nor all external, that bridge the gap between the mother's absence and her presence."[lxxxiii] My contention is that in the context of the collective changes we are living through today, Apple and some of its companion brands serve a similar function.

Today we are spellbound by Apple's imagination, and the result of this is a deep archaic identification, a "*participation mystique*" in which we find ourselves in a symbiotic if not incestuous relation to the objects of our desire on the marketplace. "In the *participation*, as in paradise, all things are woven into one."[lxxxiv] Every day, at any time, with a simple touch of our forefingers, we can symbolically transcend space, time, and everyday reality; we can escape into a fantasy of information, entertainment, and communication; we can experience splinters of magic, shadows of divinity.

4
THE MYTH OF STARBUCKS

SEPARATION

"GET ORGANIZED" is sprayed in rugged black letters over the brick facade of the nineteenth-century Gothic-style building across the street from the Starbucks Coffeehouse I'm about to enter. It is an appeal to the activists of the Occupy Wall Street movement who for months have been gathering here—a call I take personally. It awakens memories of a scribbled note that has been pinned to my refrigerator door for years: "Resistance to the organized mass can be effected only by the man who is as well organized in his individuality as the mass itself."[xxxv] Is that so? Am I getting organized? Occupying Starbucks? I plan, at least, to spend an exorbitant amount of time within its culture in order to better understand how it has transformed into the cultural icon it is today.

Opening the door, crossing the threshold, I enter into a constructed space that is unknown— but judging by its atmosphere, well-known— territory: the world of Starbucks. I am greeted by a soundscape of drifting jazz tunes and distant female voices from a long-forgotten past whispering words of love. Beans are ground, mobile conversations started, orders taken. Milk is being heated. In front of me and behind Lisa, the barista, stands—proud and silent—a siren. Encircled in green, staring seductively at me, at you, at all of us waiting in line to order, her hair seems to wave in the wind. What wind? I'm already off guard, disorganized, losing myself in daydreams, fantasies, sensory experiences. What are my objectives, again? My forefinger slides across the screen of my iPhone, opening my field notes, and I'm reminded of the questions I have set out to explore.

"What makes Starbucks the cultural icon it has become today? What gives it its unique culture? What are its myths and rituals?" Embarking on an ethnological exploration of one of the temples of globalized consumer society of the twenty-first century raises the need for clarity about a fundamental question in anthropology and its subfield ethnology: "Who is the Other?" I realize that I am saying this out loud as the woman in front of me slowly turns her head around, giving me a

disturbed smile I don't know how to meet. Who am I studying? Who is being studied? Am I being studied? There are reasons to be paranoid. This field of study, the world of Starbucks, is an entirely constructed space and experience. As consumers (of Starbucks), we are the ones being studied. You and I play the roles of "the Other" in a staged Starbucks experience. And most of us are unaware of how it is scripted.

Everything around me: I let my gaze sweep dreamily across the room, across the big art canvas portraying a single oak in an African landscape alongside the words "hope," "live your dreams," and "justice," etched as in pencil; the old nineteenth-century coffee grinders on display on the oak shelf; the large, framed, high-contrast black-and-white photos of authentically smiling coffee farmers; old sacks of coffee beans; book shelves with old nautical atlases and novels. I hear an automatic greeting from Lisa, who is waiting for my order as the groove of the beat blends smoothly into the next: it's all an expensive fantasy, an orchestrated daydream, a script for the senses written to serve the Starbucks mythology, a corporate myth that has become ritualized into an experience built on in-depth consumer studies of "the Other." What can I do but observe the observed as I am being observed? How can I hold this paradox?

"Getting organized" might not be the best strategy, after all, in this rigorously constructed field of study, at least if we want to come out of the experience with insights reaching beyond the "knowledge horizon" and what is already known by Starbucks' own consumer research department. French anthropologist Marc Augé writes in his book *The War of Dreams* that the new techniques of communication and image-making render the relation to the Other more and more abstract: "... [W]e become accustomed to seeing everything but there is some doubt whether we are still looking."[lxxxvi] To transcend the paradox and find answers to my research questions, I have chosen a strategy that is anything but organized, but rather pathological: that of the *"doppelgänger,"* the multiple personality. I have done so not in order to indulge the fancy of a seemingly psychotic researcher, but to make sure I can keep one foot—one perspective—one camera—one "I" outside the theatrical stage before me: an eye that would critically monitor the one who observes us; a macro-lens of rationality setting these experiences within the broader context of power relations and history; a complementary superego, a "directed thinker" I call Max, the personality supporting the other half of this split duo, the participant observer, Jakob, who embodies the Starbucks experience guided by his fantasy-thinking.[lxxxvii] Dear reader, please join us on this *dérive*[lxxxviii] into dreamland!

TRANSITION

"What's your name?" "Jakob," I answer, and before I realize I have given away something precious, and before I can ask her, "What for?", my name is already written, in black letters, on a white Starbucks takeaway cup and handed over to the barista. As my Visa card slides smoothly into the machine and the transaction is processed, I understand that I have just given away a part of myself, a piece of my identity, and have received in return a micro-initiation of sorts into the Starbucks culture. I start to sweat, to feel anxious, to look around nervously. Everyone is smiling, staring into space or into a screen. Somewhere someone seems to call my name.

The myth of Starbucks (official version)

Once upon a time in America, there was a self-made man named Howard Schultz working as general manager for an ordinary Swedish kitchen and houseware company outside New York. Interested in why a certain company on the American west coast named Starbucks Coffee, Tea, and Spices bought so many plastic drip filters, he decided to pay them a visit. In Seattle he was greeted by the founders, an enthusiastic threesome of relaxed west-coast academics turned coffee bean lovers and entrepreneurs. Mr. Schultz fell in love with the company and later wrote in his memoirs: "I couldn't stop thinking about Starbucks... like a jazz tune you can't get out of your head."[lxxxix]

A few years after this initial meeting, Schultz, who was already head of marketing at Starbucks, went on another trip, this time to another faraway land, Europe, where he was shot once again by the arrows of *amour*. He was in Italy for a housewares show, but instead fell in love with the Italian coffee culture, a legacy of the European coffee house tradition's romance and flair; he perceived it as great theatre. On the way back to America, he had a vision. He dreamed of transforming Starbucks from a few stores selling premium coffee beans, tea, and spices into a new type of coffee house inheriting the cultural tradition of coffee he had experienced in Italy. "We would take something old and tired and common—coffee—and weave a sense of romance and community around it. We would rediscover the mystique and charm that swirled around coffee throughout the centuries."[xc]

This is the officially approved version of the Starbucks foundation myth. It is the corporate myth that is at the heart of the Starbucks brand and that nourishes the company's vision of bringing great coffee to everyone, everywhere, one cup at a time—by offering a unique and differentiated Starbucks experience. Schultz later stated in his autobiography: "Like Nike, Starbucks had entered a low-margin commodity business and transformed its product into a cultural symbol."[xci] But how did this cultural icon find its form? What does its immense global success have to say about our collective today? In order to answer these questions, we need to look more carefully at Starbucks' history. We need to decode the brand— to de:brand Starbucks—to see how its founding mythology is translated into consumer experience. Or, speaking ethnologically, to learn how the company's mythology becomes ritualized into an act of consumption. But before that, let's return to the brand, to the heroic half of our ethnographer, our other "I." Let us rejoin Jakob on his excursion into dreamland, where he seems to have already been initiated.

"Jakob, you're Jakob, right?" I hear a voice speaking to me. Flash of a smile. Cup in my hand. Araya, the barista, is already back behind the coffee machine steaming milk and shouting, "Tall Frappuccino, extra shot, for Jennifer." I ask him: "What is this thing about the name?" He looks up, smiling before he speaks. "You know, it's about sorting out orders and all of that... it can get pretty busy here during rush hours and hard to keep track

of all the customers." He becomes silent, stares down into the cup into which, seconds into what appears to be deep meditation, he pours the foamed milk and finishes with forming the pattern of a heart before looking up to say: "Well, it's also a management thing... you know, getting to know the customer and all of that. It has something to do with getting more intimate." Finishing his sentence, he looks into my eyes again and gives me a friendly smile.

His words remind me of what Kevin Roberts, CEO of global advertising firm Saatchi & Saatchi, advised in his book Lovemarks, *that in order for brands to be competitive today, they must embrace love, which is usually accomplished by adding a trinity of mystery, sensuality, and intimacy to the customer experience. "Thanks, Araya. Now I know," I hear myself saying before I turn around, face the half-empty space, and look for my place.*

The early days: Establishing a culture

Starbucks was founded in Seattle in 1974 at a time when roller skates were the hottest thing a teenager could be on, disco music was taking over the airwaves, and *brand* was still just another word for a logotype. It was a time of rapid changes within the collective identity, which was embracing values that would stand in sharp contrast to the political revolt of the rebellious freedom-thirsty '60s, with its counterculture, student uprisings, and feminist and hippie movements. The energy of the counterculture movement began, slowly, to fade away, replaced by slogans used to sell products back to the dreamers who had inspired it. Labelled the "Pepsi generation," it would pave the way for the individualism and narcissism that would reach full bloom in the 1980s.

Imagining this lost era in social terms is integral to understanding Starbucks' legacy, how it formed its identity and corporate culture. Starbucks' three founders were all academics—intellectuals and romantics—children typical of this generation. They had escaped into the world of coffee not in search of political liberation, but on a quest for the perfect roast. Entrepreneurs (they quickly grew from one to ten stores in the area), they were motivated not by growth but by their striving for quality and "coffee perfection." They saw business as a lifestyle, a path to self-realization. They dedicated their attention to the quality of the coffee beans, teas, and spices they sold. The cappuccinos, café lattés, and colonial ambitions would come later—when Howard Schultz entered the picture.

Starbucks' first logotype is an adaptation of a sixteenth-century Norse woodcut. It was discovered by the founders' designer friend, Terry

Heckler, who stumbled upon it while searching through old marine books for nautical imagery to go with the name Starbucks (taken from the coffee-loving character named Starbuck on the ship *Pequod* in Herman Melville's novel *Moby Dick*). Encircled by the store's original name and framed in brown, it depicts a rather grim-looking two-tailed mermaid, a *Melusine*[xcii] or siren wearing a crown. "That early siren, bare-breasted and Rubenesque, was supposed to be as seductive as coffee itself,"[xciii] Schultz later wrote in his autobiography.

Sirens are, by way of the *Odyssey*, written into the canon of literary history as seductive nymphs who, with their singing and implicit promises of sex, awaken the deepest desires of men. Odysseus had his men tie him to the mast of their boat as they sailed by the sirens' island. The image of the mermaid has a sexually charged history. As early as the fifteenth century, it was used decoratively in European churches and cathedrals as a warning against temptation. But its history goes back even further, to old pagan goddess religions, where it was linked to female fertility, mystery, and power. I digress. On our own odyssey of an ethnological experiment, we will, unlike Odysseus, try to approach the Starbucks siren with open ears. We will follow her transitions and let her be our guide to the deeper, darker secrets of the Starbucks brand's mythology—the parts that did not make the official family-friendly version.

I find a seat on the upper floor with a good view over the field, right under the speaker that gives the siren its song, a steady, beating soundtrack. I put my cup down on the round wooden table that has been intentionally designed to prevent me from feeling lonely. At this point, I still don't believe that I will become familiar with this place or come back here many times over my planned weeks of study to observe the clientele, take notes, and occasionally engage in conversations.

Today is like most other days. In the room there is an average of fifteen people, as many women as men, of all ages, with the majority aged between twenty and thirty-five. They are here—on average, I estimate—for roughly one hour. An overwhelming majority are alone, sitting in front of an iMac, iPhone, or iPad, working, studying, digitally dwelling, daydreaming in front of screens. Occasionally there is someone with a book, usually a student. No one is talking to the others around us. Everyone is in her own world.

Well, today that's not really true. A person I take to be a businessman of Chinese descent is occupying the corner of the large comfortable sofa by the stairway that leads down to the first floor. He speaks loudly into the empty space in front of him. I stand up to see what's wrong with him, and from this new angle I can see his alibi, a shiny black device lying on the table. Within its frame there appears an Asian woman, I assume his wife, moving her lips as if in silent song. I feel relieved and hear myself thinking, "If there is anyone acting like a madman here, it's me." My eyes turn away, surprised by the bookshelf nearby.

Becoming a brand

The very decades—the '80s and '90s—that gave life to the Starbucks Empire would also see the company transformed into the cultural icon it has become today. "Branding" became an established practice in those decades, a practice whose mission was no longer to sell a given product, but to sell that product's image (analytically speaking, *imago*) and emotional allure. A new marketing era of *eros* had dawned, and with it a proliferation of constructions of attractive identities. "Brand personalities" and "brand experiences" became big companies' chief concerns. Like a psychological complex, the locus of branding migrated from the sensational world of advertising—slogans and billboards—to the inner world of psyche. The marketer assumed a magician's role in conjuring around products matrices of effective associations and emotional cues. Brands shifted from being mere product identifiers to becoming cultural lifestyle and status symbols, helping individuals to locate and express their own identities. Following the song of the siren, Starbucks (with Schultz at the helm)—like few other brands—would become a symbol of this new era of marketing.

In 1986, as *Top Gun* and Tom Cruise were hitting the cinemas and pop group The Bangles taught people to "Walk Like an Egyptian," Schultz had a brief extramarital affair with his enterprise Il Giornale, a chain of espresso houses he opened in frustration when it became clear to him that the original Starbucks founders did not share his dreams of coffee colonization. Only a few years later, however, Schultz would have his way when they suddenly decided to sell and Schultz took full control of the company, merging it with Il Giornale. The result of this coupling is the Starbucks we know today, a public company, no longer selling mainly coffee beans, but a retailer of espresso, café latte, giant-sized muffins, and a scripted sensorial experience: the Starbucks experience. Schultz put his foot on the pedal and accelerated into the 1990s' frenzy of brand extensions: Frappuccinos, PepsiCo joint ventures, CD compilations, instant coffee blends and espresso-flavoured ice cream. In the spirit of the times, Starbucks started selling anything but product. In 1995, there was one store in every major U.S. city. A year later, the first overseas branch opened in Tokyo. By the turn of the century they had gone from 500 to 17,000 stores worldwide.

The merger of Schultz's two enterprises led also to the development of Starbucks' logotype as we more or less know it today. The original Il Giornale logotype pictured Mercury in a green circle. In the new Starbucks version, the green image of the Roman god of speed, mercantilism, and commerce would become the picture of the Mother Goddess mermaid siren—archetypically known for her nourishing qualities and implicitly charged sexuality—now smiling post-surgery: lips lifted, all fat on her belly sucked out, airbrushed to perfection. She was a symbol at home in the celebrity-fixated *Sex in the City* culture of the 1990s. Her sexuality still being a bit much for some, a few years later, the Starbucks siren was subjected to further surgery: the removal of her navel. Symbolically, the navel represents the "lifeline," our life force.[xciv] Was the removal of the siren's navel, then, symbolic of the company's cutting away from its roots and history? A symbolic act signifying the amputation of its connection to the principles of its original founders? A tradition of cultivating low-scale coffee perfection sacrificed to commercial opportunities of coffee colonialism?

De:branding the Starbucks experience

It's mysterious. I have spent weeks coming back to

Brandpsycho

this exact spot, but I have never noticed this bookshelf before. Could it be that it is placed in a "dead" angle for me, or is it just not meant to be seen? It has three shelves and holds books of various sorts bearing a recurrent nautical theme: atlases; travel literature; older European novels with traditional binding; books people like to look at or surround themselves with, but seldom read. The thought won't leave me. Is this a real bookshelf? Is it meant to be seen? Are these books authentic, or merely stage props? Can I go up there and start casually reading one of them, or would that be breaking "the script"? Am I a virus in the scripted code of the Starbucks experience?

I abruptly stand up and walk across the room to study the shelf's contents more closely. The atlas could be interesting, I think to myself, and move my hand to take it, noticing in awe that it's glued to the book lying beneath it. I reach for another book, but it is also glued. I am filled with an anxious feeling. My heart beats faster. I start to sweat, to look around. The Chinese man is staring straight at me as his wife continues speaking; the woman behind his laptop looks up at me, her face puzzled; a group of young university students stifle their laughter. It's dead quiet. One hears only the sound of the sirens singing somewhere in the background to the beat. I get a sudden urge to explain, but I don't know how. I move back quickly toward my *seat, almost tipping a chair along the way.*

The Starbucks experience is staged for the purpose of bringing to life the romantic legacy of its mythology through stimuli touching all of the senses. Schultz explains: "We're not in the coffee business—we're in the experience business."[xcv] "The artwork, the music, the aromas, the surfaces all have to send the same subliminal message as the flavour of the coffee."[xcvi] Just like its siren, the experience carries a sensual message of seduction—the implicit promise of leaving mundane reality, an invitation to play a role in a romanticized drama of coffee house nostalgia, interpreted and staged by the brand "like theatre." Starbucks' management refers to this experience as the "third space," a place that is neither work nor home, but somewhere in between, a transitional space between fact and fiction, between dream and reality. Its founding myth has been ritualized into a consumer experience based on a careful script contrived to evoke our emotions, stimulate our senses, and lead us on a journey through a constructed imaginary echoed by the mood of the music.

At Starbucks, much like the French writer Count Xavier de Maistre in his eighteenth-century novel *A Journey Round My Chamber,*[xcvii], we are invited to travel without ever leaving the room. The novel is an autobiographical account of a young officer who, after learning, following a duel, that he is to be imprisoned in his room for six weeks, decides to start a voyage in his own chamber by travelling through fantasy. Starbucks seems to invite us on a similar journey into an imaginary land to be found on no map—all without ever leaving its branded utopia.

Brand inflation and the return of Schultz

The bustling brand frenzy of the '90s would experience, in the early days of the new millennium, a short interruption in its machinery and Minotaurian craving for growth. Naomi Klein cried "No Logo," and globalization activists turned the spotlight on the brand bullies. Schultz seemed to have run out of libido and decided to leave his post as CEO at a time when Starbucks had become a scapegoat for globalization's shadow effects. The company's problems seemed only to worsen. As Starbucks turned thirty-eight in 2008, it experienced something of a midlife crisis. The company had become too lofty and grandiose, like the Puer flying too high and too fast: "[O]pening stores became as routine as pulling shots of espresso." [xcviii] Continued Schultz in an interview with the *Harvard Business Review*: "We seemed to have become the poster child for excess."[xcix]

Starbucks' net income plummeted: over 600 stores had to be closed in the U.S. alone, and criticism continued to soar.

Coffee utopia on the threshold of dystopia paved the way for Schultz's heroic CEO comeback (perhaps rivalled only by Steve Jobs' return to Apple in 1997) in 2008. He closed down yet more unprofitable stores and set out to reinvent the distinctive Starbucks third-space experience. He sensed that the company's mythology had been watered down, and his ambition was to bring aroma, romance, theatre, and magic back to its stores. In an act as symbolic as it was practical, Schultz decided to close all Starbucks shops for half a day in order to train the staff in its corporate mythology and the technique of making a perfect espresso. The result of this and other activities was that, as of 2015, Starbucks is more successful than ever, with a market capitalization of about $81.13 billion and profits of over $11.4 billion.

Changes in the Starbucks brand are always somehow also mirrored in its logotype. In 2011, the siren was finally freed from her green circle, and in the tradition of brands like Apple and Nike before it, Starbucks' logotype dropped the company name. Why would a brand like Starbucks do this? "It gives us the freedom and flexibility to think beyond coffee,"[c] answers Schultz, who points to new ventures into categories such as energy drinks and fruit juices. Having reached the level of cultural icon means not having to write out the company name.

The Starbucks symbol has handily assumed a psychic position inside the collective hearts and minds of consumers.

RENEWAL

Opening my iMac should help me get back on script. It's a well-known accessory and status object in this milieu, and could perhaps help me re-establish some of the trust I lost with the bookshelf incident. I connect to the Starbucks wireless network. A webpage greets me with "one hour of free Internet," followed by the logo of the siren once again asking for my name. I type in "Max" this time, give away his email, and answer "perfect" to the question, "How was your coffee experience today?" I am riding the waves of the Internet, checking emails, befriending Starbucks on Facebook, following it on Twitter, and "liking" a story it has published on its blog about a guy named Dan who brought Starbucks coffee to his cancer-sick friend in Colombia. I'm the digital flâneur, a slow-surfing coffee bohemian drifting in-between physical and virtual space (reality?)—as I suddenly catch the sight of a tiny spider that has landed on top of my screen.

The (hidden) Other

The different threads of our history, woven together and looked at from a distance, portray quite a different pattern than the one presented in the official Starbucks corporate mythology. A renewed, re-envisioned, reinterpreted, and more realistic version of this corporate story cannot pretend to overlook the conspicuous link between coffee, capitalism, and its colonialist discourses. Next to oil, coffee—the black gold—is still today the world's most traded commodity. The legacy of coffee culture so proudly inherited by Schultz and the Starbucks brand not only carries elements of elegant European coffee house romance, but is also embedded, more implicitly, in practices of power, exploitation, and slavery.

The purpose of this ethnological experiment is not to highlight and critique the already well-documented post-colonization project or the omnipresence of Starbucks Coffee in today's increasingly globalized (and as a result, gentrified) world. Rather, the purpose is to better understand the unconscious psychic connection we as postmodern consumers have built with the brand—thereby putting the spotlight on an underlying and potentially more alarming psychological colonization: that of our imagination. When we try now to stitch together the two perspectives of the *doppelgänger* Jakob and Max—micro and macro, fiction and fact, dream and reality, ethnological observation and historical decoding—a more complex pattern emerges. We are left, if not with something as aesthetically pleasing, at least with a more realistic image of the siren's face.

If we are to believe Starbucks' own management about what has transformed the brand into a cultural icon, we would concede that the key lies in how the company has managed to ritualize its founding mythology into a differentiated third-space experience. It has romanticized and mystified coffee culture, taken a low-margin commodity and turned it into an experience consumers are willing to pay more for (and come back for). Our ethnological observations, combined with historical decoding of the brand—its experience and symbolism—reveal that there are deeper powers at play. For Marc Augé, "all ritual activity has the goal of producing identity through the recognition of alterities."[ci] He writes that, seen anthropologically, "[t]he question of identity is always posed in relation to *the other*."[cii] This leads us back to our initial, until now unanswered, question of "who" and "what" that *Other* is? Who is the Other Starbucks consumers form their identities in relationship to?

At first glance, the Other seems to be others, our fellow consumers on the market stage, the people with whom we interact and to whom we communicate our social status and differentiation via our choice of brand consumption. More importantly, though, the hidden Other in relation to which we form an identity is the Starbucks brand itself, injected as it is with "mana" by its management and mythmakers. In a dance of mutual projection between (unconscious) consumers and the (conscious) Starbucks brand— by embodying their constructed mythology ritualized into a brand experience—we form an "imagined consumer identity," a lifestyle ghostwritten by Starbucks.

Our selves take form in what sociocultural anthropologist Arun Appudai describes as a "mediascape," which, for the purposes of this chapter finale, we rename "brandscape." "Mediascapes... tend to be image-centred, narrative-based accounts of strips of reality... out of which scripts can be formed of imagined lives..."[ciii] As this ritual is performed repetitively, a deep form of identification appears to take hold, reminding us of what ethnologist Lucien Levy-Brühl called *participation mystique.* Levy-Brühl used the term to describe how "primitive cultures" form a symbiotic relationship with objects, a relationship that, according to Marie-Louise von Franz, is characterized by "a minimum of self-awareness combined with a maximum of attachment to the object."[civ] What are the cultural consequences of this continuously repeated and increasingly global psychological drama?

The myth of Starbucks (revised)

I am perplexed by the intrusion of this archaic little arachnid that seems as confused as I am and to have spent too much time in this space. I observe the fragile thread it spins, a hanging bridge between my screen and the empty chair opposite. "How long have you been here?" I imagine him asking and myself answering, "For a month," before I realize that I am about to lose it completely, have lived in this fantasy for too long. But the symbolism of the spider has caught my (unscripted) imagination. In Buddhist philosophy, the spider spins māyā, the veil of the world built up out of illusions. In mythology it is seen as a manifestation of the cosmic creator and demiurge. In psychoanalysis it symbolizes the devouring mother and her related complexes, which can draw the analysand into a comfortable web of childhood fantasies of omnipotence, an oceanic feeling of nostalgic longing amounting to an escape from real-life responsibilities: stuck in adolescence, forever young, utopia become dystopia. I carefully pick up the thread and release the link between us, understanding that it's time for me to leave.

Schultz writes in his autobiography that his "highest aim is to have... the entire Starbucks experience provide human connection and personal enrichment in cherished moments around the world, one cup at a time."[cv] Our ethnological observations contradict this conscious wish. The Starbucks experience is a highly individualized one, characterized by a lack of human interaction. Prominent in our ethnological observations was the intensive use of digital communication technologies, smart phones, and screens, and an overall sense of alienation and separation between people, each person in his own world. Marc Augé uses the term "non-places" to designate "spaces of solitary individuality"[cvi] and disconnection, such as airplanes or motor highways, where individual identity is lost. Is Starbucks such a non-place? Or perhaps it's a non-state?

Seen with these suspicious eyes, Starbucks is the symbol of a globalized utopian state, not limited by any national borders. Ubiquitously it transcends geography, not only in its global colonization of physical space, but also in its psychological conquest of the imagination. The word *utopia* is rooted in Greek and Latin and can be translated as "no-where," a "no-place-land," a form of "unreal reality," a land of imagination that is both distant and close. As we repetitively perform the Starbucks ritual of consumption, we seem to be offered a subliminal promise of transcendence of the inherent paradoxes of our biological and postmodern existence.

Is one of the reasons for Starbucks' success

that the company offers new solutions to address the problem of "liquid modernity"?[cvii] A non-place between work and home for the globalized consumer? A non-state in which stoic philosopher Seneca's warning that "[t]o be everywhere is to be nowhere"[cviii] seems to have been outpaced by the ubiquitous postmodern ideal of being always connected? Emotionally alienated from other people, we are constantly embedded in a comforting and nourishing web of sensual fantasies, technological transcendence, and oral satisfactions stimulated by the mother—sorry, market.

Hey, I'm still here! Don't leave me. I am looking for the exit but seem to have gotten lost. All the spaces I have spent time in, all the weeks that have passed by, seem to have blurred into one. "Did I occupy? Was I occupied?" I think to myself as a green sign informs me that THIS IS NOT AN EXIT. I turn around, now in a rush to leave, dizzy with flashes of familiar faces staring relentlessly into screens and of the barista who always smiles, takes my name but never remembers it. In my head the sirens sing an endless echo. There is no turning back, I think, as I finally spot the door, approach and open it. Air! Inhale. Exhale. Closing my eyes, I breathe slowly. Opening them again, right in front of me a tram rushes by carrying an ad that someone has tagged with a black marker:

UNFUCK THE WORLD. "A good reason to get organized?" Max asks as we cross the street.

EPILOGUE

Separation. Leaving the branded self of psychological identification with collective ideals and one's own persona means turning away from off-the-shelf fantasies sold on the market. It means shifting one's attention away from artificial dreamscapes to inner dream realities. It means beginning to reconnect again with one's own media-making machine: one's own imagination. It is a painful process involving the loss of all-encompassing market fantasies and an encounter with the inner, unwanted, uncared-for sides of our nature.

Here they are, the dirty, difficult, depressed parts of the self that seldom get any Facebook likes. Boredom. Anxiety. Panic attacks. Like? No, I did not think so, but these are all common psychological reactions when facing the very serious process of change and personal transformation, when facing the Other in ourselves, the one who did not "make the cut" of the shiny persona we worked so hard to present to the world. "It's not a game anymore," a voice whispers as we encounter the wasteland of our own soul, the spiritual malaise of the consumer culture we have internalized. We stand small now, alone, like a scared animal blinded by mere mortality, facing our finiteness and limitations. Naked as the brands we have so playfully undressed. Here begins a lonesome walk through a dried-out desert. Here begins facing the void that is the precondition for all human imagination.

Turn yourself into an experiment

Jung wrote that the aim of his therapy was "... to bring about a psychic state in which my patient begins to experiment with his own nature—a state of fluidity, change, and growth where nothing is eternally fixed and hopelessly petrified."[cix] An individual's process of change can begin when everything one previously understood to be reality loses its foundation, when all truths become challenged. The psychoanalytic relationship can, at its best, be a laboratory containing such self-experiments. It is a simple yet radical setting in which, if one is committed, one's alliance with the analyst can help create the environment necessary for the formation of a new identity—an identity freed from mass-media ideals and the imperatives of the branded self—based on a connection to one's "I," which is a precondition for relating authentically to the Other and the collective.

Psychoanalysis on the street

A colleague recently told me that psychoanalysis is going crazy in a controlled environment. It seems to me today that there is an increasing desire in individuals to share at least some form of craziness together with others. In Berlin, where I have my psychoanalytical practice, the most awe-inspiring rituals created for madness, which for the ancient Greeks belonged to a separate Dionysian realm, are to be found in the eclectic club culture. The techno clubs are our secular temples of dance and desire, where people perform self-experiments through drugs and sexual experimentation.

In the analytical room and in my clients' dreams, one club in particular comes up again and again. Berghain is the church of clubs in Berlin and has, in these last decades, been the mecca for self-experimenters in the city. It is a club as famous for its ecstatic DJ sets as for its strict door policy and dark rooms (no cameras allowed). The club seems to offer some of the people in this city a Dionysian outlet and communal stage for experimenting psychologically, for going crazy with others. It is an alternative dream to the brand utopia promoted by the marketplace. But it is a dream that seems at times to risk losing its psychological and soulful dimensions, which involve making sense and meaning of one's experiences. Leaving the party, depleted of endorphins, facing the daylight, one comes down from one's high, from yet another peak experience, with no real change having taken place. In order for change to occur, it has to stick. Psychological experiments like these need to become embodied in body and mind, spirit and soul. The club experience often lacks what the encounter with a solid analyst can realize: a deeper connection with one's self, a sense of awe for psyche, a possible meaningful change of attitude and perspective.

But psychology, particularly psychoanalysis, needs the club. It needs techno, strobe lights, the communal ecstasy that the club experience offers at its best. For psychology has, also in recent decades, retreated into the politics of individualism perpetuated by capitalist economics. It has become solipsistic in its preoccupation with diagnostics, fixing and adapting "sick" individuals to help them become more productive within the system. It has at times become a means of re-branding people, of normalizing and balancing them, of reabsorbing them into the system as de-politicized individuals endlessly seeking pleasure and well-being.

Psychology today has repressed its communal

and social ethos. It has forgotten what it once was. Psychoanalysis as initiated by Sigmund Freud was a cultural movement that emerged not only to treat neurotic individuals but to study and present hypotheses about how culture can make us so sick. And psychoanalysis as rendered by Carl Jung was not only about finding yin-yang balance and a connection with one's true self, which is what it has become in its New Age iteration. No, it was an idea about how mythology, history, and the collective past continue to live through every human being— about how forces beyond our own individual powers animate our actions and shape our individual lives. Up until the Second World War, before psychoanalysis went into exile, it was truly out on the streets of Europe. Pioneering psychoanalysts such as Wilhelm Reich, Otto Gross, Karen Horney, Otto Fenichel, Sabina Spielrein, Sándor Ferenczi, and Karl Abraham carried a fire set not only to transform the individual psyche but the collective itself.

In my fantasy, the one I have shared with you in the essays in this book, psychoanalysis and psychology hit the streets again. There, clients and practitioners alike start to bring psychological perspective to their surroundings. Look around! It's alive: the consumer products, the houses we build, the cars we drive, the way we commute. It's all animated by psyche. When we de:brand consumer icons and mass-media images, we withdraw some of the psychic energy we have outsourced to the companies that own them and thereby us. We stop seeing and treating ourselves as products, which are all that is left of brands when they too are stripped of human attributes.

REFERENCES

Aaker, Jennifer L. "Dimensions of Brand Personality." *Journal of Marketing Research* August (1997): 347-356. Print.

"A Look at the Future of Starbucks." Perf. Howard Schultz. 7 March 2011. *Starbucks.com*. Starbucks Corporation. Web. 1 July 2015. <http://www.starbucks.com/preview>.

Appadurai, Arjun. "Disjuncture and Difference in the Global Cultural Economy." *Education, Globalization, & Social Change*. Ed. Hugh Lauder et al. Oxford and New York: Oxford UP, 2006.

"Apple Keynote: The '1984' Ad Introduction." Dir. Ridley Scott. Perf. Steve Jobs. *The Apple History Channel*. 1 April 2006. *YouTube*. YouTube, LLC. Web. 1 July 2015. <http://www.youtube.com/watch?v=ISiQA6KKyJo>.

Auden, W.H. "We are Lived by Powers We Pretend to Understand." 29 January 2011. *Verbal Medicine*. Rick Marshall. Web. 26 July 2015. <http://rickmarshall.blogspot.de/2011/01/we-are-lived-by-powers-we-pretend-to.html>.

Augé, Marc. *The War of Dreams: Exercises in Ethno-Fiction*. London, VA: Pluto Press, 1999.

Baudrillard, Jean. *Simulacra and Simulation*. Trans. Sheila Faria Glaser. Ann Arbor: University of Michigan Press, 1994.

Bauman, Zygmunt. *Liquid Modernity*. Cambridge: Polity Press, 2000.

--. *Postmodern Ethics*. Oxford: Blackwell, 1993.

Beck, Aaron T. *Cognitive Therapy and the Emotional Disorders*. New York: International Universities Press, 1976.

"Brand." *Online Etymology Dictionary*. Douglas Harper, 2001-2015. Web. 1 July 2015. <http://www.etymonline.com/index.php?term=brand>.

Broughton, Philip Delves. *The Art of the Sale: Learning from the Masters About the Business of Life*. New York: Penguin Press, 2012.

Campbell, Joseph. *The Hero with a Thousand Faces*. Novato, CA: New World Library, 2008.

Cawthorne, Bianca. *The Power of Archetypes in Brand Creation* [PowerPoint presentation]. 20 September 2009. *SlideShare*. Web. 1 July 2015. <http://www.slideshare.net/biancacawthorne/the-power-of-archetypes-in-brand-creation>.

Chevalier, Jean and Alain Gheerbrant. Trans. John Buchanan-Brown. *The Penguin Dictionary of Symbols*. London: Penguin Books, 1996.

"Consumer." *Online Etymology Dictionary*. Douglas Harper, 2001-2015. Web. 1 July2015. <http://www.etymonline.com/index.php?term=consumer&allowed_in_frame=0>.

Cushman, Philip. *Constructing the Self, Constructing America: A Cultural History of Psychotherapy*. Reading, MA: Addison-Wesley, 1995.

Davies, Andrea and Richard Elliott. "Symbolic Brands and Authenticity of Identity Performance." *Brand Culture*. Ed. Jonathan Schroeder and Miriam Salzer-Mörling. Oxon and New York: Routlege, 2006.

Defining Magic: A Reader. Ed. Bernd-Christian Otto and Michael Stausberg. Sheffield; Bristol, CT: Equinox, 2013.

Dell, Paul F. and John A. O'Neil. *Dissociation and the Dissociative Disorders: DSM-V and Beyond*. New York: Routledge, 2009.

Dichter, Ernest. *The Strategy of Desire*. Garden City, NY: Doubleday, 1960.

Ellenberger, Henri F. *The Discovery of the Unconscious: The History and Evolution of Dynamic Psychiatry*. New York: Basic Books, 1970.

Festinger, Leon. *A Theory of Cognitive Dissonance*. Evanstan, IL: Row & Peterson, 1957.

-- *When Prophecy Fails: A Social and Psychological Study of a Modern Group that Predicted the Destruction of the World*. New York: Harper & Row, 1964.

Fierz, Heinrich Karl. *Jungian Psychiatry*. Einsiedeln: Daimon Verlag, 1991.

Freud, Sigmund. "Civilization and Its Discontents." *The Standard Edition of the Complete Psychological Works of Sigmund Freud, Volume XXI (1927-1931)*. New York: Norton, 1961.

Heilbrunn, Benoît. "Brave New Brands: Cultural Branding Between Utopia and A-Topia." *Brand Culture*. London and New York: Routledge, 2006.

Hertzfeld, Andy. "Reality Distortion Field." February 1981. *Folklore.org*. Andy Hertzfeld. Web. 1 July 2015. <http://www.folklore.org/StoryView.py?story=Reality_Distortion_Field.txt>.

Heuer, Gottfried. "Jung's Twin Brother: Otto Gross and Carl Gustav Jung." *The Journal of Analytical Psychology* 46(4) (2001): 655-88. Print.

Hillman, James. *The Essential James Hillman: A Blue Fire*. Ed. Thomas Moore. London: Routledge, 1990.

--. *The Thought of the Heart; and the Soul of the World*. Dallas: Spring, 1992.
Ignatius, Adi. "We Had to Own the Mistakes." July-August 2010. *Harvard Business Review Online*. Harvard Business Publishing. Web. 13 July 2015. <https://hbr.org/2010/07/the-hbr-interview-we-had-to-own-the-mistakes/ar/1>.

"It's Time for Bill Gates to Come Back to Microsoft." 26 May 2011. *Engadget*. AOL Inc. Web. 1 July 2015. <http://www.engadget.com/discuss/it-s-time-for-bill-gates-to-come-back-to-microsoft-dqz/>.

Kaplan, David A. "Howard Schultz Brews Strong Coffee at Starbucks." 12 December 2011. *Fortune.com*. Time Inc. Web. 1 July 2015. <http://fortune.com/2011/11/17/howard-schultz-brews-strong-coffee-at-starbucks/>.

Kimbles, Samuel L. and Thomas Singer. *The Cultural Complex: Contemporary Jungian Perspectives on Psyche and Society*. Hove, East Sussex and New York: Brunner-Routledge, 2004.

Jobs, Steve. "You've Got to Find What You Love, Jobs Says." 14 June 2005. *Stanford University Online*. Standford University. Web. 13 July 2015. <http://news.stanford.edu/news/2005/june15/jobs-061505.html>.

Jung, Carl G. *Letters*. Ed. Gerhard Adler and Aniela Jaffé. 2 vols. Princeton: Princeton UP, 1973.

--. *The Collected Works of C.G. Jung*. Ed. Sir Herbert Read et al. Trans. R.F.C. Hull. Vols. 1-20. New York: Princeton UP, 1970-1979.

--. "The 'Face to Face' Interview." *C.G. Jung Speaking: Interviews and Encounters*. Ed. William McGuire and R.F.K. Hull. Princeton: Princeton UP, 1977.

--. *The Red Book: Liber Novus*. Ed. Sonu Shamdasani. New York: Norton, 2009.

Lebow, Victor. "Price Competition in 1955." *Journal of Retailing* 31.1 *Spring* (1955): 5-10. Print.

Lusensky, Max Jakob. "Did You Bite the Magic Apple?" *Jung Journal: Culture & Psyche* 8:1 (Winter 2014): 57-70. Web. 12 July 2015. <http://www.tandfonline.com/doi/full/10.1080/19342039.2014.841445#abstract>.

Malinowski, Bronislaw. *Magic, Science, and Religion*. Garden City, NY: Doubleday, 1954.

Markoff, John. *What the Dormouse Said: How the Sixties Counterculture Shaped the Personal Computer Industry*. New York: Viking, 2005.

Maslow, Abraham. "A Theory of Human Motivation." *Psychological Review* 50(4) (1943): 370-96. Print.

"May the Giant Be With You." *Twin Peaks*. ABC. 30 September 1990. Television.

McLuhan, Marshall. *Understanding Media: The Extensions of Man*. Toronto: McGraw-Hill Paperbacks, 1965.

Melzer, Annabelle H. *Dada and Surrealist Performance*. Baltimore and London: John Hopkins, 1994.

Noble, David F. *The Religion of Technology: The Divinity of Man and the Spirit of Invention*. New York: A.A. Knopf, 1997.

Orwell, George. *Nineteen Eighty-Four: The Complete Works of George Orwell*. Ed. Peter Davison. Vol. 9. London: Secker & Warburg, 1997.

Schultz, Howard. *Pour Your Heart Into It: How Starbucks Built a Company One Cup at a Time*. New York: Hyperion, 1997.

Seneca, Lucius Annaeus. *Letters from a Stoic: Epistulae Morales ad Lucilium*. Trans. Robin Campbell. Harmondsworth: Penguin, 1969.

Stein, Murray. *Jung's Map of the Soul: An Introduction*. Chicago: Open Court, 1998.

Tacey, David. "Jung and the New Age: A Study in Contrasts." Ed. Mary Ann Holthaus. *Jung 2.0*. No date. No publisher. Web. 12 July 2015. <http://www.jung2.org/ArticleLibrary/taceyd1.pdf>.

The Freud/Jung Letters: The Correspondence between Sigmund Freud and C.G Jung. Ed. William McGuire. Trans. Ralph Manheim and R.F.C. Hull. Princeton: Princeton UP, 1974.

Tolstoy, Leo. *A Confession and Other Religious Writings*. Trans. Jane Kentish. Harmondsworth: Penguin, 1987.

Valiunas, Algis. "Psychology's Magician." *The New Atlantis: A Journal of Technology and Society* Spring (31) (2011): 93-121. The Centre for the Study of Technology and Society. Web. <http://www.thenewatlantis.com/docLib/20110824_TNA31Valiunas.pdf>.

Von Franz, Marie-Louise. *Projection and Recollection in Jungian Psychology: Reflections of the Soul*. Trans. William H. Kennedy. La Salle, IL: Open Court, 1980.

Weber, Max. "Science as a Vocation." *From Max Weber: Essays in Sociology*. New York: Oxford UP, 1958.

Žižek, Slavoj. *The Plague of Fantasies*. London and New York: Verso, 1997.

i Leo Tolstoy, *A Confession and Other Religious Writings*, trans. Jane Kentish (Harmondsworth: Penguin, 1987) 25.

ii This line appears in the following episode of *Twin Peaks*: "May the Giant Be with You," *Twin Peaks*, ABC, 30 September 1990, television.

iii Carl G. Jung, "Commentary on 'The Secret of the Golden Flower,'" *The Collected Works of C. G. Jung*, ed. Sir Herbert Read et al., trans. R.F.C. Hull, vol. 13 (New York: Princeton UP, 1968), 20 vols., 1953-79, par. 54.

iv W.H. Auden, "We are Lived by Powers We Pretend to Understand," 29 January 2011, *Verbal Medicine*, web, 26 July 2015 <http://rickmarshall.blogspot.de/2011/01/we-are-lived-by-powers-we-pretend-to.html>.

v Max Weber, "Science as a Vocation," *From Max Weber: Essays in Sociology* (New York: Oxford UP, 1958) 139.

vi Jung, Preface, "On the Psychology of the Unconscious," *Collected Works*, vol. 7, 5.

vii Henri F. Ellenberger, *The Discovery of the Unconscious: The History and Evolution of Dynamic Psychiatry* (New York: Basic Books, 1970) 672.

viii Jung, *The Red Book: Liber Novus*, ed. Sonu Shamdasani (New York: Norton, 2009) p. vii.

ix Zygmunt Bauman, *Postmodern Ethics* (Oxford: Blackwell, 1993).

x Annabelle H. Melzer, *Dada and Surrealist Performance* (Baltimore and London: John Hopkins, 1994) 55.

xi Jung, *Collected Works*, vol. 11, par. 8.

xii Jung, *Collected Works*, vol. 11, par. 6.

xiii Jung, *Collected Works*, vol. 11, par. 9.

xiv Jung, "The 'Face to Face' Interview," *C.G. Jung Speaking: Interviews and Encounters*, ed. William McGuire and R.F.C. Hull (Princeton: Princeton UP, 1977) 428.

xv Jung, *Letters*, ed. Gerhard Adler and Aniela Jaffé, 2 vols. (Princeton, Princeton UP, 1973) 377.

xvi Jung, "On Psychic Energy," *Collected Works*, vol. 8, par. 110.

xvii Jung, "On the Psychology of the Unconscious," *Collected Works*, vol. 7, par. 399.

xviii *The Freud/Jung Letters: The Correspondence between Sigmund Freud and C.G. Jung*, ed. William McGuire, trans. Ralph Manheim and R.F.C. Hull (Princeton: Princeton UP, 1974) 156.

xix *The Freud/Jung Letters*, 153.

xx Cited in Gottfried Heuer, "Jung's Twin Brother: Otto Gross and Carl Gustav Jung," *Journal of Analytical Psychology* 46 (4) (2001): 670.

xxi Heuer, "Jung's Twin Brother," 670.

xxii Heuer, "Jung's Twin Brother," 660.

xxiii Bronislaw Malinowski, *Magic, Science, and Religion* (Garden City, NY: Doubleday, 1954).

xxiv David Tacey, "Jung and the New Age: A Study in Contrasts," ed. Mary Ann Holthaus, *Jung 2.0*, n.p., n.d., web, 12 July 2015 <http://www.jung2.org/ArticleLibrary/taceyd1.pdf>.

xxv Jung, *Collected Works*, vol. 8, par. 747.

xxvi Ernest Dichter, *The Strategy of Desire* (Garden City, N.Y.: Doubleday, 1960) 86.

xxvii Dichter, *The Strategy of Desire*, 86.

xxviii Dichter, *The Strategy of Desire*, 86.

xxix Jung, *Collected Works*, vol. 8, par. 89.

xxx Jung, "Concerning Rebirth," *Collected Works*, vol. 9.1, par. 215.

xxxi Jung, "Concerning Rebirth," *Collected Works*, vol. 9.1, par. 215.

xxxii Abraham Maslow, "A Theory of Human Motivation," *Psychological Review* 50(4) (1943): 370-96.

xxxiii Jung, "Flying Saucers: A Modern Myth," *Collected Works*, vol. 10, par. 624.

xxxiv John Markoff, *What the Dormouse Said: How the Sixties Counterculture Shaped the Personal Computer Industry* (New York: Viking, 2005).

xxxv Marshall McLuhan, *Understanding Media: The Extensions of Man* (Toronto: McGraw-Hill Paperbacks, 1965) 21.

xxxvi Cited in McLuhan, *Understanding Media*, 21.

xxxvii Sigmund Freud, "Civilization and Its Discontents," *The Standard Edition of the Complete Psychological Works of Sigmund Freud, Volume XXI (1927-1931)* (New York: Norton, 1961) 35.

xxxviii Murray Stein, *Jung's Map of the Soul: An Introduction* (Chicago: Open Court, 1998) 39.

xxxix Here we follow Jung's definition of neurosis as a symptom of maladjustment and disunity with oneself; it is a dissociation in the individual activated by complexes, but also an attempt at self-cure and healing on the part of the unconscious psyche.

xl Projection is an automatic process whereby the contents of one's own unconscious are perceived to be in others. For a more detailed explanation, see *The New York Association for Analytical Psychology Online*, 2005-11, web, 12 July 2015 <http://www.nyaap.org/jung-lexicon/p>.

xli "Brand," *Online Etymology Dictionary*, 2015, web, 1 July 2015 <http://www.etymonline.com/index.php?term=brand>.

xlii "Consumer," *Online Etymology Dictionary*, 2015, web, 1 July 2015 <http://www.etymonline.com/index.php?term=consumer&allowed_in_frame=0>.

xliii Victor Lebow, "Price Competition in 1955," *Journal of Retailing* Spring (1955): 7.

xliv The concept of the "branded self" derives both from Jung's concept of persona (identification, the collective within) and Freud's ideas about the superego (the internalized other, the part of the mind that copies external objects, the part of the personality that is closest to being an object).

xlv Slavoj Žižek, *The Plague of Fantasies* (London and New York: Verso, 1997) 39.

xlvi Zygmunt Bauman, *Liquid Modernity* (Cambridge: Polity Press, 2000).

xlvii Stein, *Jung's Map of the Soul*, 83.

xlviii Jennifer L. Aaker, "Dimensions of Brand Personality," *Journal of Marketing Research* 34(3) (August 1997): 347-356.

xlix Dichter, *The Strategy of Desire*.

l Samuel L. Kimbles and Thomas Singer, *The Cultural Complex: Contemporary Jungian Perspectives on Psyche and Society* (Hove, East Sussex and New York: Brunner-Routledge, 2004) 6.

li See Bernard Cova and Veronique Cova, "Tribal Aspects of Postmodern Consumption Research: The Case of French In-Line Roller Skates," *Journal of Consumer Behaviour* 1(1) (2001): 67-76.

lii Andrea Davies and Richard Elliott, "Symbolic Brands and Authenticity of Identity Performance," *Brand Culture*, ed. Jonathan E. Schroeder and Miriam Salzer-Mörling (Oxon and New York: Routledge, 2006) 155-6.

liii See also Max Jakob Lusensky, "Did You Bite the Magic Apple?" *Jung Journal: Culture & Psyche* 8(1) (Winter 2014): 57-70, web, 15 July 2015 <http://www.tandfonline.com/doi/full/10.1080/ 19342039.2014.841445#abstract> .

liv James Hillman, *The Thought of the Heart; and the Soul of the World* (Dallas: Spring, 1992) 96.

lv Hillman, *The Thought of the Heart; and the Soul of the World*, 101.

lvi Algis Valiunas, "Psychology's Magician," *The New Atlantis: A Journal of Technology and Society* Spring (31) (2011): 107.

lvii Hillman, *The Thought of the Heart; and the Soul of the World*, 96.

lviii Benoît Heilbrunn, "Brave New Brands: Cultural Branding Between Utopia and A-topia," *Brand Culture* (London and New York: Routedge, 2006): 107.

lix George Orwell, *Nineteen Eighty-Four: The Complete Works of George Orwell*, ed. Peter Davison, vol. 9 (London: Secker & Warburg, 1997) 224.

lx Paul F. Dell and John A. O'Neil, *Dissociation and the Dissociative Disorders: DSM-V and Beyond* (New York: Routledge, 2009) xx-xxi.

lxi See Jean Baudrillard, *Simulacra and Simulation*, trans. Sheila Faria Glaser (Ann Arbor: University of Michigan Press, 1994).

lxii Heilbrunn, "Brave New Brands," 104.

lxiii Orwell, *Nineteen Eighty-Four*, 223.

lxiv Orwell, *Nineteen Eighty-Four*, 37-8.

lxv See Aaron T. Beck, *Cognitive Therapy and the Emotional Disorders* (New York: International Universities Press, 1976).

lxvi See Leon Festinger, *A Theory of Cognitive Dissonance* (Evanstan, IL: Row & Peterson, 1957).

lxvii Leon Festinger, *When Prophecy Fails: A Social and Psychological Study of a Modern Group that Predicted the Destruction of the World* (New York: Harper & Row, 1964).

lxviii David F. Noble, *The Religion of Technology: The Divinity of Man and the Spirit of Invention* (New York: A.A. Knopf, 1997).

[lxix] James Hillman, *The Essential James Hillman: A Blue Fire*, ed. Thomas Moore (London: Routledge, 1990) 206.

[lxx] Malinowski, *Magic, Science, and Religion*, 84.

[lxxi] "Apple Keynote: The '1984' Ad Introduction," dir. Ridley Scott, perf. Steve Jobs. *The Apple History Channel*, 1 April 2006, *YouTube*, web, 1 July 2015 <http://www.youtube.com/watch?v=ISiQA6KKyJo>.

[lxxii] "Apple Keynote: The '1984' Ad Introduction," 1 July 2015.

[lxxiii] Steve Jobs, "You've got to find what you love, Jobs says," 14 June 2005, *Stanford University Online*, web, 13 July 2015 <http://news.stanford.edu/news/2005/june15/jobs-061505.html>.

[lxxiv] See Shunryu Suzuki, *Zen Mind: Beginner's Mind*, ed. Trudy Dixon (New York: Weatherhill, 1970) 1938.

[lxxv] See Joseph Campbell, *The Hero with a Thousand Faces* (Novato, CA: New World Library, 2008).

[lxxvi] Bianca Cawthorne, *The Power of Archetypes in Brand Creation* [PowerPoint presentation], 20 September 2009, *SlideShare*, web, 1 July 2015 <http://www.slideshare.net/biancacawthorne/the-power-of-archetypes-in-brand-creation>.

[lxxvii] Malinowski, *Magic, Science, and Religion*, 70.

[lxxviii] Andy Hertzfeld, "Reality Distortion Field," February 1981, *The Original Macintosh*, web, 1 July 2015 <http://www.folklore.org/StoryView.py?story=Reality_Distortion_Field.txt>.

[lxxix] "It's Time for Bill Gates to Come Back to Microsoft," 26 May 2011, *Engadget*, web, 1 July 2015 <http://www.engadget.com/discuss/it-s-time-for-bill-gates-to-come-back-to-microsoft-dqz>.

[lxxx] Malinowski, *Magic, Science, and Religion*, 75.

[lxxxi] Philip Delves Broughton, *The Art of the Sale: Learning from the Masters About the Business of Life* (New York: Penguin Press, 2012) 99-100.

[lxxxii] James Frazer cited in *Defining Magic: A Reader*, ed. Bernd-Christian Otto and Michael Stausberg (Sheffield; Bristol, CT: Equinox, 2013) 82.

[lxxxiii] Philip Cushman, *Constructing the Self, Constructing America: A Cultural History of Psychotherapy* (Reading, MA: Addison-Wesley, 1995) 257.

[lxxxiv] Heinrich Karl Fierz, *Jungian Psychiatry* (Einsiedeln: Daimon Verlag, 1991) 215.

[lxxxv] Jung, "The Undiscovered Self," *Collected Works*, vol. 10, par. 540.

[lxxxvi] Marc Augé, *The War of Dreams: Exercises in Ethno-Fiction* (London, VA: Pluto Press, 1999) 14.

[lxxxvii] A term launched by Carl Gustav Jung, fantasy-thinking is a thinking that is guided by unconscious motives. Jung writes in *Collected Works*, vol. 5, par. 20: "Almost every day we can see for ourselves, when falling asleep, how our fantasies get woven into our dreams, so that between day-dreaming and night-dreaming there is not much difference. We have therefore two kinds of thinking: directed thinking, and dreaming or fantasy-thinking. The former operates with speech elements for the purpose of communication, and is difficult and exhausting; the latter is effortless, working as it were spontaneously, with the contents ready to hand, and guided by unconscious motives."

[lxxxviii] *Dérive*, literally "drifting," is a term developed by the activist group Situationist International and their main theorist Guy Debord for explaining a technique of rapid passage through varied ambiances. In a *dérive* one or more persons during a certain period of time drop their relations, their work and leisure activities, and all their other usual motives for movement and action, and let themselves be drawn by the attractions of the terrain and the encounters they find there.

[lxxxix] Howard Schultz, *Pour Your Heart Into It: How Starbucks Built a Company One Cup at a Time* (New York: Hyperion, 1997) 38.

[xc] Schultz, *Pour Your Heart Into It*, 77.

[xci] Schultz, *Pour Your Heart Into It*, 262.

[xcii] *Melusine* or *Melusina* is a feminine spirit of fresh waters that lives in sacred springs and rivers, a well-known figure of European folklore, legends, and myths. Usually she is depicted as a woman who is a serpent or fish from the waist down, much like the mermaid.

[xciii] Schultz, *Pour Your Heart Into It*, 33.

[xciv] Jean Chevalier and Alain Gheerbrant, *The Penguin Dictionary of Symbols*, trans. John Buchanan-Brown (London: Penguin Books, 1996) 719.

[xcv] David A. Kaplan, "Howard Schultz Brews Strong Coffee at Starbucks," 12 December 2011, *Fortune*, web, 1 July 2015 <http://fortune.com/2011/11/17/howard-schultz-brews-strong-coffee-at-starbucks>.

[xcvi] Schultz, *Pour Your Heart Into It*, 252.

[xcvii] Xavier de Maistre, *A Journey Around My Room* (London: Hesperus Press, 2004).

[xcviii] Schultz, *Pour Your Heart Into It*, 193.

[xcix] Adi Ignatius, "We Had to Own the Mistakes," July-August 2010, *Harvard Business Review Online*, web, 13 July 2015. <https://hbr.org/2010/07/the-hbr-interview-we-had-to-own-the-mistakes/ar/1>.

[c] "A Look at the Future of Starbucks," perf. Howard Schultz, 7 March 2011, *Starbucks.com*, 1 July 2015 <http://www.starbucks.com/preview>.

[ci] Augé, *The War of Dreams*, 11.

[cii] Augé, *The War of Dreams*, 10.

[ciii] Arjun Appadurai, "Disjuncture and Difference in the Global Cultural Economy," *Education, Globalization, & Social Change*, ed. Hugh Lauder et al (Oxford and New York: Oxford UP, 2006) 183.

[civ] Marie-Louise Von Franz, *Projection and Recollection in Jungian Psychology: Reflections of the Soul*, trans. William H. Kennedy (La Salle, IL: Open Court, 1980) 9.

[cv] Schultz, *Pour Your Heart Into It*, 266.

[cvi] Marc Augé, *Non-Places: Introduction to an Anthropology of Super*

Modernity (London and New York: Verso, 1995) 75-115.

[cvii] Liquid modernity is a term used by sociologist Zygmunt Bauman to define a postmodern state of fluid existences seeking identity in a globalized and individualized world predominated by digital communication technologies. The postmodern identity is seen as individually constructed in a continuous reflexive and dynamic process with one's environment.

[cviii] Lucius Annaeus Seneca, *Letters from a Stoic: Epistulae Morales ad Lucilium*, trans. Robin Campbell (Harmondsworth: Penguin, 1969) 33.

[cix] Jung, "The Aim of Psychotherapy," *Collected Works*, vol. 16, par. 99.

Made in United States
North Haven, CT
07 December 2023

45242255R00068